A Workbook For Mastering Awareness of Perceptual Positions & States

Healing Strategies for Narcissistic Injuries & Illusions

A 60 Hour Continuing Education Course
Offered by
Eclectic Therapy Press

Tobias S. Schreiber, M.A., LPCS, NBCCH, NCC
Wilton L. Hellams, PhD., LPCS, NBCCH
June 25, 2009

This workbook is dedicated to my wife *Laine Schreiber* for all her love, support, and encouragement. Also in my thoughts are our children, Brad, Chris, Joy, Kristie, Marie, and Joshua Tobias, grandchildren Jamie, Nicholas, Joshua, Heather, Jacob, Christa, Skyler, Callie, Zoë, Tyler, Landon, Aeden, Owen, Jadyn and Sims.

My business partner Wilton Hellams has been a steadfast friend along with his family, which includes his wife Roberta, his son, Jeremy, and his daughter Emily.

My clients, supervisees, and colleagues have inspired me to seek ways to teach and share my journey into the world of identity creation.

Stephen Wolinsky with his example and encouragement brought me to the teachings of Sri Nisargadatta Maharaj, which opened a universe of the Absolute.

"May your heart be uplifted and your path endlessly peaceful, as the embrace of the infinite lifts your song to the winds of the timeless."

© *2009*

All rights reserved. No part of this book may be reproduced in any manner whatever, including information storage, or retrieval, in whole or in part (except for brief quotations in critical articles, or reviews), without written permission from the publisher.

ISBN# 978-0-578-03192-7
Eclectic Therapy Press
274 Summerfield Road
Moore, South Carolina 29369-8918
www.eclectic-therapist.com

Chapter Outline

Chapter 1. Mapping for Everyone	1
Chapter 2. What a Personal Journey Can Reveal	3
Chapter 3. Mapping Construction	5
Exercise: for Feelings	**9-10**
Chapter 4. From Mayberry to Baghdad and Back Again	12
Chapter 5. Awakening	14
Chapter 6. Creating and Experiencing The "I"	18
Exercises for Identities	**24**
Chapter 7. Creating and Un-creating The "I"	25
Chapter 8. Moving from Identity to The Witness	28
Chapter 9. Yoga & the Consciousness	30
Tree of Life Illustration	32
Exercises for Conceptual Lens	**33**
Chapter 10. Sensory Perceptual Identification Alignment	37-56
Exercise: Present Time Sensory Alignment	**41**
Conceptual Frameworks I	44
Conceptual Frameworks II	45
Enneagram- 9 False Fixations and Their Compensators	**46**
Chapter 11. Loss of Essence	48
Exercises: Strategy Questions for Identities	52-53
Exercise: Discovering the False Core	**54**
Exercise: Processing the False Core	**55-56**
Chapter 12. Essence and the Therapy Of Presence	57

III

Chapter Outline

Chapter 13. Trance Phenomena	59-74
Chapter 14. Programming Errors	74-85
Chapter 14. Identity Creation Illustration:	86
Identity Loop	99
Exercise: Questions for Identities	**100**
Semantic Reversal	101
Chapter 15. The Diamond of Awareness	**104**
Exercise: Time	**117**
Exercise: Assume, Decide, Or Believe	**118**
Illustration	120
Illustration: Diamond of Awareness	127
Exercise: Thoughts	**128**
Exercise: Location	**132**
Exercise: Identities	**133**
Illustration: Life of Life's Terms	136
Illustration: Acceptance and Map Alignment	137
Trance Disruption Techniques	138-163
Chapter 15. The Flame and Light	164
For the Therapists	166-177
Chapter 16. **Movement of Energy in the Body**	153
	178-179
Appendix:	
15 Styles of Distorted Thinking	182-183
Chevreul's Pendulum	184
Facts*Stories*Experiences	185
Family Development Dynamics	186

Chapter Outline

Indirect Forms of Suggestion	187-191
Levels of Consciousness	192
Categories of Memory	193
Autonomic Nervous System	194
Organization of the CNS	195
Post Hypnotic Suggestions	196-198
Postulates for the Creed of Eclectic Therapists	199-202
Sensory Words	203
Sample Suggestions	204
Sub-Modality Distinctions	205-207
Six Step Re-Framing	208-209
The Structural Development Continuum	210
Therapeutic Use of Trance Phenomena	211
Visual, Auditory, Kinesthetic Word List	212-213
Visual-Kinesthetic Dissociation	214-215
Visual Squash	216
Swish	217
Key Terms	218-221
Bibliography	**222-231**

Are you tired of being unhappy?

Are you sick of running into dead ends and roads that lead you nowhere?

Are you weary from struggling to find a sense of calm?

Have you been experiencing the roller coaster of emotional ups and downs?

Do you feel as if life is driving you, rather than you directing your life?

If the answer to one or more of these questions is, yes. You can find the answers to your freedom and success here in this book on "Sensory Perceptive Mapping".

Turn the page to begin revealing the secret of these simple answers already contained within your mapping system.

Mapping for Everyone

A Personal Journey

Each of us is on an amazing journey into the world of our personal lives. As infants, we had no idea what would lie before us, or the wonders that we would see or experience. Before we could undertake this journey, an interesting transformation would take place. We were all hypnotized into believing that we must forget who we are, and become someone else. We would be indoctrinated into the strange beliefs of the adults and others that we lived with and we were dependent upon. One thing that some of us were taught is that you should not think of yourself or be selfish. Another thing that you might have been told was that often what we were feeling or thinking was incorrect and that we should not think feel, speak or act on what we were experiencing. So over time we were taught to distrust or discount what we think and feel, and look outside of ourselves for the answers about what we should think, feel and do. We are told marvelous stories and myths about what we can become and how to have relationships and be valuable. Some of us experience childhood as a nightmare from which we must escape, while others experience it as if it were a fairytale and they are princes or princesses. Some children are treated well and others are like slaves to the despots who rule a hard and difficult world. Much of what we experienced in our particular childhood depends on who we lived with and what their beliefs were about life and about children. We all lived in a world with people who were bigger than we were, they were the givers of pleasure and pain, they controlled the food supply and told us where and when to sleep. The most benign ruler still wants his or her own way. So, what was your experience, and what ideas and beliefs did you develop from and through your childhood? We have ideas about whom and what our parents were and are. We were able to observe our parents or caregivers and although children are good observers they have an undeveloped ability to interpret and give meaning to what they see, hear and experience. As I attempt to describe the various possibilities of what we may have experienced I am reminded of what Korzybski stated when he said, "You can always say more about what you've already said, and still add nothing to it."

When things do not go the way you want, you look for the reason. As has been demonstrated with Bell's Theorem in Quantum physics causality is an illusion. The search for cause is the nervous system's attempt to create a Universe that is *knowable, predictable, and controllable.* This is a way that the *Sensory Perceptive Holographic Mapping System* can create a world that it can navigate. Therefore, when you feel alone, separate, imperfect, worthless, powerless, loveless, non-existent, or anything as a lack, you decide this is the cause of the loss or failure. In order to overcome the *false cause* you overcompensate and create a *false solution*, such as being more perfect, more lovable, more worthy and so forth. There is the continuous struggle to resolve, re-enact, recreate, resist, or re-enforce this imagined weakness or flaw, which in fact does not exist, except in the mind of the individual.

What a Journey Can Reveal

Now, let us continue our exploration of the self and its mapping system by joining a group of friends preparing for an adventure. Imagine for a moment that you and several friends have decided to go on a trip for fun, learning, and self-discovery. Each person involved is hoping that the experiences will reveal new things to enhance their life. Therefore, they decide that rather than taking a trip by boat, plane, motorcycle or some other form of transportation that this trip will be by car. Rather than traveling to a foreign destination our group of travelers will be leaving from Charleston, South Carolina and making their way to Los Antes, New Mexico. Each member of the group has contributed suggestions for various sites to visit as they make their way to the final destination. As the group of friends meets to plan the route they will travel, each shares information about the route from their preferred source of traveling information. One person consulted a travel agent and has a custom-made map, another has an old travel guide that they rely on when going on a trip, and another traveler has purchased a new GPS satellite guidance system. Each of them trusts in their own method of navigating the territory before them. All of the sources of information claim to be accurate representations of the terrain that the travelers will be encountering.

As you might expect each of the friends has different ideas about what they might see and experience on this adventure. In order to coordinate, the trip they make a list of the different places they will stop and visit as well as the type of activity and the amount of time that needs to be allotted for each individual excursion. Each of our travelers has their unique ideas about what will be important for them on this journey. Learning, adventure, challenges, comfort, excitement are all poured and stirred into the mix. Some of the adventurers are very visual and look forward to the sites, colors and contrasting scenery. Others are much attuned to the sounds that they will be exposed to and the things they will be hearing about from the accents of a particular area, musical sounds of the area or the local history recited by the storytellers. The various fragrances of the flowers or restaurants of the locality are of great interest. The cuisine of the area is an exciting opportunity for the travelers to taste the seasoning and variety of vegetables and fare of the local cooks. Deciding whether to camp in the countryside visit a bed and breakfast or stay in a five star hotel is still up for consideration. For now, the travelers' minds are not thinking about work, the route to the mall two blocks away, or the knowledge that meteors are flying through space. They are totally focused on the mission before them.

The journey has begun and they have been traveling for several days when much to their surprise and consternation the road before them is blocked by newly begun construction and all traffic has been re-routed. They find that they are frustrated and confused by these changes in their plans. Each of the friends begins to give reasons and explanations why their map is not congruent with the actual territory. They struggle internally with their own tendency to hold on to their beliefs about the correctness of their map. It is with great effort that they realign their maps with the territory; however, during the process they provide many unique and interesting explanations for the inaccuracies of their maps. They discuss ways that they have been deceived or how they really are correct after all. Some of them feel strange or uncomfortable as if they are out of their comfort zone or element. These are the affects of *homeostasis* as they maneuver us into giving up realizations or new information or behavior. Change is difficult because the system resists it in favor of sameness and predictability. However, you can influence the affects of *homeostasis*, by recognizing it for what it is and persisting in the changes you seek. In the works of *Neuro Linguistic Programming*, this would be called an *ecological check*. That is, you would do an internal scan and ask the question "Is there any part of me that has any objection to this proposed change?" This questioning is to make sure that the entire organism is in harmony with the proposed change and that all parts of the organism are heard and respected.

Mapping Construction

As you, begin to explore how our mapping system is constructed. We are going to explore the various elements that make up maps and their representation of the territory/world. Mapping is an ongoing interactive representational system that attempts to assist the organism in navigating the world. Much like the GPS systems we use to guide us as we travel in our cars, the mapping system guides us in traversing the thoroughfares of our daily lives. The mapping system uses the tools of our senses as the way to replicate and represent the territory it is attempting to describe. Within the mapping system are visual, auditory, tactile, kinesthetic, gustatory, and olfactory representations of the experiential territory. Along with the representations are the names, references, associations, and meanings of these objects. The organism's nervous system attempts to organize the chaos as the energy flows through the energetic, cellular field of the organism. Keep in mind that the world, the stimuli that activate the senses, the effects upon the nervous system, the resulting representations, the categorization, as well as the singular, contextual meanings and the resulting responses that the information may have may have some imagined causal connection. Now, as you begin to take notice of the ways that you use and are aware of the various elements in your personal mapping system, you can also notice you are mostly cognizant of the sensory system or yourself when you focus on it for some reason. Let's begin to explore the ways we sense and represent the stimulus world. Keep in your awareness that although we are compartmentalizing the various elements and their aspects, this is simply for convenience and ease of discussion, for there are complex interactions within and throughout these elements.

Visual Elements: Visual stimuli come in an array of shades, colors, hues, and brightness. Visuals can be bright, dull, near, or far way. The images can be crisp and clear or ambiguous. The images can be foreground, background, figure, or ground. There are images that are generated by stimulus from the external environment, there are images that are internally generated remembrances or recreations from previous experiences, and then there may be images that are combinations of internal and external interactions. As you create or notice some image, regardless, of whether it is, *internally generated or externally stimulated, notice where the image is located in the visual space, whether it is to the right, the left, the center, the front, the back, high, or low. You might also be curious to find out what if anything occurs if you alter the location, the distance, the size, brightness, or color.* Remember what the mind (nervous system) creates it can change or un-create. *Take notice of an image and then become aware of the space that it is floating in. Now, what would occur if you were to realize that the image and the space are made of the same substance?*

Sounds or Auditory Elements: Like images, sounds can be internally created or derived from the interpretation of external stimuli. Sounds can be simply sounds like the wind, leaves falling, cars starting, brakes scraping and millions of other sounds. Music is a sound that mixes different instrumental sounds or voices. We may hear sounds that have a *tone*, a *timbre*, a *tempo*, a softness, loudness, far away or close. Sounds can be singular or it can be a particular person's voice. Voices can be in a general or certain context. *Take a moment to notice the various types of effects sounds have on you. Perhaps you can notice how you remember a particular individual's voice and how you respond to that sound.*

Tactile or touch elements: Textures and a plethora of tactile sensations affect the body when they are sensed. External and internal sensations alert the organism to notice what is occurring in its space. Touch can acquaint us with our environment and it can inform us of pleasures and pains. Various aspects of touch give us a sense of our physical form and information about temperature, weather and sense of our physical dimensions.

Kinesthetics: Kinesthetics give us information about the internal state of the organism as it responds energetically to the stimuli that flow in, around, and through it. Heart beats, respiration, muscle contraction or elongation as the body responds to the stimulus world.

Taste Elements: Sweet, sour, hot, mild, salty, spicy and an almost endless variety of taste. Taste gives us ore information about a complex sensory world with salty, sweet, acidic, metallic taste that not only stimulates the taste buds; it informs the body of the chemical content of the food.

Smell Elements: The olfactory sense is quite powerful and can transport you to another place or another time when you first encounter it. Scent is powerful and yet subtle. Scent informs one of changes in the environment; whether it is some toxic gas that endangers the individual, smoke from a charcoal grill with seafood, steak or barbequed ribs or even the gentle scent of flowers in the spring. It could even be a forest fire in the distance.

Associational and Referential Elements: The way that one sense relates to another or the way that it connects and brings meaning to our experiential world is amazing. We develop ways of categorizing and differentiating the myriad of sensations in our stimulus world. Each of the senses can be explored individually but it is a masterful mosaic that is created by the intricate interweaving of all the senses to create our life experience. We describe the mapping system as holographic to convey the idea that it is multi dimensional, multi sensorial, and interactive system. By exploring and utilizing the various editing and altering functions of this sensory representational system, you can begin to discover how one part of the system influences and affects another. One aspect of the system is the interaction of thoughts, feelings, and actions. Each of these represents an element that can be dealt with separately but can act in unison.

Thoughts: Thoughts are the by-product of sensory stimulation. Thoughts appear from the emptiness (space) and resolve, return into the space.

Thoughts are like clouds drifting in the sky and your consciousness is the space they are floating in. The thoughts are just thoughts, although, you may think or feel they are your thoughts. Just as your walk in between the people on a crowed sidewalk, so you can walk in between the thoughts that appear in the mind. Do not resist the thoughts; just allow them to do what they do. Sometimes you can objectify the thoughts and see them as if they are floating in the sky. Then, *you can realize that they are made of the same substance as the sky.*

Feelings: The body does at least two things: production of energy is the first, and the use of energy is the second. Feelings represent the energetic orientation of the organism to the sensory stimulus. Thinking of attraction (approach) and avoidance the positions are: approach-approach, approach-avoidance, and avoidance-avoidance. We are moving towards the stimulus, away from the stimulus or we are energetically ambivalent to the stimulus. Ambivalence = "ambi" or *equally* "valence" or *charged + or -* in relation to the object.

Exercises for Feelings:

1. a. Allow a feeling to come into your awareness.

    b. Now, notice where in your physical space you experience the feeling.

    c. Notice if there is a story or explanation that goes with that feeling. If there is, take your mind off of the story, and just experience the feeling.

    d. Notice the label you have for that feeling, take the label off, and just have it as energy.

    e. Now, let the energy do what the energy does.

2. a. Let a feeling arise.

   b. Notice what label or name you have given it.

   c. Notice where in your physical or mental space you are experiencing the feeling.

   d. Step into the feeling, and notice the size and shape of the feeling.

   e. What occurs if you allow the feeling to expand?

   f. What if it were the size of the room, the state, the world?

   g. **Remember to breath, and stay present at each experience.**

   h. Notice at what point it *dissipates*.

   i. Notice the space the feeling is floating in, and then ask yourself this question. *"If the space and the feeling are made of the same substance what occurs?"*

Keep in mind that there are very often several layers of feelings before you reach the original. Chronic *anger* often covers or masks *pain* or *fear*.

Feeling are real, however they are often based on inaccurate information.

The feelings we have about a particular object or experience may be a blend of past associated feelings with present feelings.

Feelings being chemical responses will take some time to resolve or process and allow the body to return to its previous resting state. So, keep in mind that once an emotional state is initiated even if we discover our information was wrong we will still experience the chemical reaction that has begun until it dissipates.

If you discover that once in an experience that it is difficult to step out of it, it indicates that you are overly associated with the experience and may need to burn off the energy by experiencing it more. If you find it difficult to step into an experience then you may be disassociated from the experience.

Actions: Movement and interaction is the result of sensory information directed toward the survival of the organism. The body organizes and mobilizes its resources by creating, utilizing and directing its energy.

Energy, Mass, and Space-Time:

Each of these elements has dimensions of Energy, Mass, and Space-Time. Everything in this universe exists in energy, mass, and space-time and the things that we experience in this universe all share elements of energy, mass, and space-time. All things have a time that they exist in. All things have duration. All things whether they are objects or thoughts have a mass or density. They can be ethereal or massive. Everything has a space that it occupies and moves in or through. All things exhibit energy whether it is weak or strong.

Mapping

Maps are tools that assist you in locating where you are, where you are going and where you may have been. Some maps are designed with certain goals in mind while others are created to be used in a general way to determine location and to plot out a course of travel. You can decide your own destination, or the trip may be predestined. Maps can be topical, multi layered, simple, or intricate in their representation of the territory we seek to describe. We develop historical maps, time maps, anatomical maps, territorial maps, and an almost endless array of maps depending on our need.

From Mayberry to Baghdad and Back Again (The Map of Trauma, War and PTSD)

Princes into frogs, The Fall from Grace and other Mythical Misconceptions and Stories of the how we came to be where we are and the way we can reclaim our Birthright

We continue, by following our theme of Sensory Perceptive holographic mapping as the way in which all of us move through and recognize our world. This representational system assists in recognizing familiar sights sounds, sensations as well as including taste and smells. The gentle breeze on a summer or fall morning, the sound of children in a park or the smell of popcorn at a movie is all things that bring associations of memories of comfort and a world known in a hometown. This is vastly different from the map that is created for the soldier thrust into the world and experience of war. The sights, sounds, smells sensations, and tastes of a world that exist in a parallel yet different time and place. We discover a place on the same planet but with experiences unfamiliar to the peaceful lives and dreams of everyday citizens.

Bill relays a story of a time he experienced coming to the awareness that he was in the living room of his father's home with a shotgun pointed at his father , and realized he needed to torque it down a notch . He had recently returned from Marine duty in an area of high security and high risk. Someone had not turned the alarm off that night and it accidentally went off. Bill now reacted with lightening speed to ensure his survival and safety, but that is the mapping of another time and place and completely unnecessary and out of place in the present location. In fact, it could be dangerous and quite disturbing to others who are unfamiliar with the places and experiences that Bill has seen and that are now a part of his associations when stimuli occur.

The Elvis phenomenon is an example of the Gestalt Closure principle, where people are hoping to see someone or something and you get numerous random sightings. There are also reports of ghosts, Alien abductions, Big Foot, the Loch Nest Monster and a whole host of other things that people report with no verification.

What is normal? Normal is the setting on a washing machine as well as being an abstract concept that tricks all of us into believing that it is something that we should aspire to. In counseling, we move individuals that are struggling with conforming to the societal norm toward this imaginary guideline.

Awakening to:
What Isn't, Wasn't, and Will Never Be

As consciousness manifest as a mind/body there is the essence of possibility that is within the space. Through the interaction of the biological organism and the environment the experiential concept/filter called the *person* begins to be formed without will or awareness. The created person is of little use to the absolute/infinite because it is interested and engaged in a struggle and quest created from its own imaginings fueled by the biology, genetics, hopes, dreams, and myths of the other imaginary beings that fill the universal dream. There may come an age of awakening where there will be the opportunity for the awareness to begin to focus its observing ability in a neutral way to discover how to free itself from the cycle of 'Maya' and 'illusion'.

The finger pointing at the moon is not the moon, be careful that you do not become distracted and miss the real vision. Reflections in the water are images but they are not the person. We create images of who we wish to be or imagine that we are. A life time can be spent creating an illusion that has no more substance than smoke on the mountain easily blown away by the wind or dissipated by the warmth of the sun at morning. What appears to be a solid personality is in reality a *persistent pattern of trance clusters*, which appears when there are stimuli present that create an interactive focal point much like a vortex. In the Supreme Yoga a wise statement challenges us to understand the true nature of what is experienced,

> "This world-appearance is a confusion; even as the blueness of the sky is an optical illusion, I think it is better not to let the mind dwell on it, but to ignore it."

Focusing on the illusion can create amnesia for the focusing consciousness so that it merges or fuses with the identity. Remind yourself that you will only suffer to the degree that you believe you are your identities. Identities are limited focal points in space-time, they are not who you are they are tools for filtering experiences.

> *"A weak mind cannot control its projections. Be aware, therefore, of your mind and its projections. You cannot control what you do not know. On the other hand, knowledge gives power. In practice, it is simple. To control yourself-know yourself."* Sri Nisargadatta Maharaj, I Am That, 1973)

There is a Sanskrit saying that is useful to keep in mind as it relates to the *Identity* and the *sensory perceptive holographic mapping system* or the world of the person. The saying is *Dristi, Shristi, Vada*, "The world is only there as long as there is an "I" there to perceive it." (The Supreme Yoga, Swami Venkatesananda, 1976). As we begin to explore the identities that appear and disappear within the *mapping system* keep in mind that the map is not the territory and the identity is not the person.

> ***"This is the mystery of imagination that it seems to be so real. You may be celibate or married, a monk or a family man; that is not the point. Are you a slave to your imagination or are you not? Whatever decision you take, whatever work you do will invariably be based on imagination, on assumptions parading as facts."*** (*I Am That*, Sri Nisargadatta Maharaj, 1973).

Each time you find your awareness captured by an identity, remember it is a concept, it is not you. So tell yourself, *"As I experience things through this point of view created by the effects of this (**X**), "Martyr" identity I will stay aware it is not me."* As you feel the effects of each identity you will know its gravitational pull and feel as if you could sink into it, you may even find it difficult, not to experience things without its distorting influence.

An interesting statement to meditate on is the idea or concept that *"a crow alights on the coconut palm tree and that very moment a ripe coconut falls. The two unrelated events thus seem related in time and space, though there is no causal relationship.*

Such is life. Such is 'creation'. But the mind caught up in its own trap of logic questions 'why', invents a 'why' and a 'wherefore' to satisfy itself, conveniently ignoring the inconvenient questions that still haunt an intelligent mind." As is found in this injunction we find that through the concept of the *Sensory Perceptive Holographic Mapping System* and its need to produce 'knowledge' about itself, the world and the interactions so that it can *know*, *predict* and *control* the movement and flow of the imaginary scenarios that it imposes on its projection on the canvas of energy, mass and space-time.

'**You can have it as you like. You can distinguish in your life a pattern or see merely a chain of accidents. <u>Explanations are meant to please the mind. They need not be true.</u> Reality is indefinable and indescribable.**'

You can view the world/universe experience through any created position you choose, however, keep in mind that they are all created and are maps or conceptual frameworks. '*For the purpose of discussion you can arrange words and give them meaning, but the fact remains that all knowledge is a form of ignorance. The most accurate map is yet only paper. All knowledge is in memory; it is only recognition, while reality is beyond the duality of the knower and the known.*' {Sri Nisargadatta Maharaj, I Am That}.

Maharaj once said, *"I am speaking from the Absolute position, the name of the talk is spiritual talk, the name of the game is cards."* With observation you will discover that all of your activities, spiritual, worldly and otherwise are merely activities to pass the time.

Creating and Experiencing the 'I"

There are a variety of reasons an individual could be interested in dealing with identity structure, the creation of the "I" and ways to deconstruct the "I" and increase awareness and flexibility in the focusing of attention. The narcissistic delusion and illusion is to believe that the lens or map that one views and experiences the world and the self through is real and has a life to be lived. The myth of the person is like all myths based on the stories, hopes, dreams, imagination and narratives of the family, culture and location of the person. And although it is tied up in our ethos, it is not true. As Dr. Stephen Wolinsky stated **I** + anything (Statement, concept) = Identity. **I** + image + meaning= the creation of a storyline for the "I" to live out and pursue. When you add *infantile grandiosity* which is the idea, belief that I am the center of the universe and deserve to have what I want, and *magical thinking*, which is the belief that if I want something bad enough I can have it, you create an ongoing drama which is the personal life. Another complication is the failure to individuate, where the person is still dependent on others to decide and support who they are. When you are not yourself, you cannot decide independently what you need to do, who you should be, or what to join or be a part of. Incompleteness in an individual's individuation leaves them vulnerable to the influences and distortions of others. One of the nervous system's primary goals is the survival of the organism and one way it tries to complete this task is by having *knowledge* about what is going on. *Knowing* is situation, and time limited although the nervous system attempts to generalize one experience to another. It is said in the Vedas that "knowledge is bondage." This means that whatever you know about something limits what else you could know or discover. Also, Sri Nisargadatta Maharaj said, "Whatever you know about yourself came from outside of you, discard it." *Knowing*, *predicting* and *controlling* are some of the methods the nervous system uses to try and regulate the movement of life and be in charge of the outcome. Life is made up of a series of endless *activities* some more enjoyable than others, all equally meaningless. We label the activities, giving them levels of importance that are contrived. The nervous system seeks to give experiences and perceptions meaning and further give it a form and so it creates information. Applying the experience of one event to another often generates mis-information. *Mapping misapplications* or *mapping mis-transpositions* occur when we attempt the apply learning from one person to another or one event to another, one time to another, one location to another. It is certainly wise to notice how things occur, however "*you cannot put your foot into the same river twice*", and so it is with experiences. Experiencing different views by noticing the lens, maps or filters we are applying helps to keep us awake and aware. Gurdjieff once said that we are engaged in the war against sleep. Maharaj said that when we are unaware we suffer, so, if we do not wish to suffer, we need to stay awake. So, one purpose of awareness exercise would be to loosen the "*Samskaras*" or mind impressions. These are the tendencies of the mind to see hear, feel, smell, taste and respond to experiences in a particular way. It is also as Milton H. Erickson, M.D. said that *therapeutic trances were to depotentiate the conscious set*, which is the ongoing daily trance. Loosening the structure of the mental mapping system is a concept that unpacks or frees up the ways we frame our understandings. You use a thorn to remove a thorn and then you throw it away. You use a concept or frame of reference to remove other frames of reference or concepts. To step in and out of perceptual positions teaches one to notice that all positions are just positions. Experience the micro and macro view, experience being no-thing and then experience being everything. Maharaj said that "wisdom says that I am nothing, and love says that I am everything and between these two my life flows." Then also experience the non-dual self which encompasses both and all, but is neither. Maharaj once stated that he discovered that *"spirituality is as discard-able as dishwater."* I take this to mean that it cleans or washes away the debris of our false learnings and concepts and then it too must be washed away. So, these exercises and experiences give you opportunities to freely notice and become aware of the impact and effects of various conceptual frameworks and perceptual positions which you can view the existence through but they are not the existence or appearance. "Wear the uniform do not become the uniform", do not forget who you are.

As you begin to work on the awareness of perceptual positions keep in mind that all location is relative to position or vice-versa. How you choose to locate your awareness in energy, mass and space-time is determined by the representational position that gets created. This position can be created in awareness or out of awareness. Some perceptual positions are learned before or without articulation and therefore, can be without conscious interactive awareness. Examples are things parents or caregivers could have modeled for us when we were young children or infants. Positions are conceptual frameworks or abstracted representational locations in space-time and as such have all the elements and attributes of energy mass and space time. This means that a position may have a certain density or mass as well as movement, force and gravitational pull or repulsion. The position may occupy a specific location in space time, be that mental or physical and may also have duration or length of time.

Things that have appearance in this universe share the elements known in the universe, light force, dark force, associations, etc. As a wise teacher said, *"there is no birth, there is no death, there is no person, it is all a concept, it is all an illusion, and now you know the nothing and you can leave."* Sri Nisargadatta Maharaj. (Personal conversation with Stephen Wolinsky, PhD) There is only **no** substance, because if there were one or more substances there would have to be something separate from it to say it was one. The "I" is the original conceptual position and from there the concepts and creations are endless. This not to say it is good or bad, right or wrong, simply that it is not. Even space and time do not exist but are creations within the imaginary I am. As we begin to investigate the consciousness, allow yourself the flexibility to experience and un-experience all the various conceptual positions. True freedom as my friend and teacher Dr. Stephen Wolinsky stated means *"free to have it, as well as, free to not have it"*.

One way of experiencing things is to objectify them, and even thoughts, feelings, behaviors, beliefs, philosophies and other ideas and experiences can be objectified. The human experience is grounded in the body or at least the concept of a body and its mind, which watches over and protects it. As we are well aware there is no separate body and mind, there is one organism. The concepts of science, philosophy, religion and society are represented by the ideas of Descartes who divided the body and mind. Notice that whenever you become aware of the body it is always here, it is never anywhere else. The time the body exists is always now and so, it appears that the body is always here and now. The conceptual mind however, is always somewhere else or in some other time such as in the past or future. The body responds to stimulus in the here and now, but the mind stimulates the body with pictures, thoughts and sensations that may be from any location or time. Noticing the nature of the thoughts, images, and sensations may prove interesting. By noticing them you can step back from them like passersby on the sidewalk or clouds drifting in the blue sky. You can turn any thought, image, or sensory impression into an object to be observed. **Homeostasis** is the gyroscope that rights the sensory perceptive holographic mapping system. Objects at rest tend to stay at rest; homeostasis ensures that change is not done without its influence.

The power of homeostasis is noticed anytime change is attempted. You can notice a sense of discomfort, or an inner voice criticizing the new behavior, questioning the need or wisdom of the choice. That voice may seem to be a parent, a teacher, or someone of influence.

Notice for yourself the infinite number of ways some part of you intervenes when you attempt change, for good or ill.

When exploring thoughts, images, feelings, beliefs, philosophies, concepts or identities you can notice the following:

Examples of things to be observed, objectified, experienced, un-experienced, created, and uncreated are as follows:

Thoughts: positive thoughts, critical thoughts, negative thoughts, sad thoughts

Feelings: Sadness, Happiness, Fear, Anger, Shame, Guilt, Worry, Sexual feelings.

Images: people, places, things, [memories of the past, present, future].

Sensations: smells, taste, sounds, the wind, sunlight

Sensory Impressions: a flower, a person, sunset, snow, ice cream

Beliefs: truth, God, fairness, good, democrat, republican

Philosophies: Buddhist, Judeo-Christian, Existential, Humanitarian

Identities: man, woman, counselor, parent, father, mother

Exercises: for Identities

Does the **X** have energy? Does it seem fast, slow or frozen? Are you drawn to **X** or is it drawn to you, or neither? Are you repelled by **X**, Is **x** repelled by you or neither?

What is the size or shape of the energy or its absence? Does the energy have a color? Does it stay the same or change? Does it have a temperature?

Where does the energy start? Where does it go? How does it move? How does the energy stop or does it stop and disappear?

Notice the energy. Give it a label that describes it, then peel back the label and notice what is underneath or behind it. Notice that, and continue this process until there is nothing coming up.

Another exercise is to let the energy expand, larger and larger, noticing the effects at each stage of expansion or change. Notice any denial, resistance or lack of energy.

Notice the space **X** occupies. Is it thick or thin, heavy or light or neither? Does the space have a color? Is there a label over the space? Notice the size and or shape of the space. Notice any labels attached or associated with or to the space. Notice any lack of space.

Notice if **X** has mass? What is the size, shape, and or density? What are the associations to X and how are they connected?

Is there a time that **X** exists? Is there a time X doesn't exist? How long does it exist? Is X in time or beyond time? Notice if there is a beginning, middle and end? Notice any absence or denial of time.

> As you begin to notice the time there are many questions that can be explored. How do you code time? Does the time appear in front of you from right to left and can be viewed as scenes through your life or does the timeline run from behind you with you standing in the *present* and looking forward to the future. Time can be viewed in scenes or as events in time. Or things can be viewed in time. Questions such as:
>
> A. In relation to **X** what was? In relation to **X** what is? In relation to **X** what will be?
>
> B. In relation to **X** what was not? In relation to **X** what is not? In relation to **X** what won't be?

Creating and Un-creating the "I"

The manifestation of consciousness is similar to the loading of a computer in that the system boots up and has the basic capabilities of consciousness without any identification, the loading of the supporting programs, peripheral systems and a central operating system are necessary for the identity to begin its development. The basic sensory system is integrally intertwined with the central nervous system which simultaneously monitors the internal state of the organism as well as the location of the organism in relation to the sea of the infinite it is in. Initially there is no-one present inside the body mind; however, over-time as the sensory impressions assimilate and ameliorate there begins to be an orienting to the various stimuli whether it is to attract or to repel or being neutral in its charge. For a time the information is not in relation to the developing identity. The guidance is from external organisms and, so, the development is unarticulated and what could be called unconscious or other conscious. The *"samskaras"* or impressions as they are called begin the creation of what we call the *sensory perceptive holographic interactive mapping system* and as such make up the foundational impressions that give the person the tendency to act in a particular way. The initial impressions are sensory impressions that are given the chemical and Neuro-physical propensity to respond in an idiosyncratic manner when presented with stimuli; however it does not dictate the exact manner of response, but is a tendency. Depending on the various genetic interactions and the biochemical permutations the organism's unique presentation is further influenced by interaction with the mother, father, other caregivers, family, community, and a myriad of environmental variations that are entered into the complex equation that generates responses. Indoctrination and induction into the various response sets solidifies the parameters of the mapping system and its seamless development. Homeostasis or the tendency toward sameness and what appears to be balance has wielded its guiding influence from the onset. Homeostasis is apparent in everything from the body temperature at 98.6 degrees, to goose pimples to restrict the loss of body heat when chilled on a cool morning. The ability to sweat in order to prevent the overheating of the body when energy use increases during exercise or labor. This also extends to the boundaries of the sensory perceptive mapping system and its assimilation, accommodation and synthesis of the sensory impressions that bombard the developing entity. The homeostatic mechanism has the ability to adjust the sensory stimuli, to adapt it and use it in a way that conforms and is in harmony with the pre-existing representational hologram. Generalizing, distorting, deleting, creating, and confabulating are all ways the senses stay congruent with the balance of the sensory representation of itself and its interaction with the expanding universe. Awareness occurs and there is no-one watching witnessing occurs and there is no witness. Consciousness takes form and receives a name and it is **"I"**. Along with the birth of the *"I"* the universe appears. A life and a life plan are soon developed and then the unfolding saga of a conceptual life begins. The individual begins the work of biological development and within a short period of time the socialization process begins. The social constraints of how, when, where and in what manner needs can be met or if they can be considered at all is quickly put into operation. Eventually the person has a life, but from time to time upheavals occur that create questions, opportunities for reflection and wondering about who and what we are.

As Ramana Maharshi the Indian Saint, once said to a seeker, who wanted to find who he was and end his suffering. You must *"go back the way you came."* You must find the source of the **I**. Between the clear consciousness and the world there is a barely detectable screen, filter or portal. The conceptual "I" is an abstracted representational filter that alters things so that there is an *experiencer* and the *experienced*. Actually if you step back from the filter you will notice that there is really only *experiencing*. Initially you start out as *unknowing*, then there is *awareness* with *no I*, then there is the *witness*, (I without words) a subtle shift in focus brings one to the *observer*, a step beyond the observer is the *I*, and then the *person* and various *identities* or *roles/sub identities*.

So, in order to free the consciousness from its imagined self created prison you must go back the way you came. You must find your way back through the various positions of drama, emotions, beliefs, identities, observers and witnesses. The only real question is, "who do you imagine, pretend, or believe that you are?" and who told you that?

Moving from Identity to The Witness

Become aware of Witnessing--- Then notice how there is Awareness—- Shift the Focus of Attention- and become Conscious of the following:

> **Curiosity/danger**
> **Light**
> **Air**
> **Temperature**
> **Body/Sensations**
> **5-Senses**
> **Pressure**

Observing – can be Internal/External -------- No Labels/No identity

Observer Identity----------- Label

Identity-------creates meaning – orientation of -- sensation---feeling

Label   Body/Mind

Approach/Avoidance is the energetic orientation of the body/mind

Awareness/consciousness

Merge------------ self-remember/experience ------ detach --------- flow

Merge-------self-forget/experience--- ⟲ Fuse Resist ⟲ Block in flow

                                 Notice alterations in Space
                                 Notice alterations in Time
                                 Notice alterations in Energy
                                 Notice alterations in Mass
                                 Notice alterations in Associations
                                 Notice alterations in Sensations
                                 Notice alterations in Thinking
                                 Notice alterations in Feeling

All experiences are in a state of *transmutation;* notice how you resist/deny transmutation/change.

Space is always the same space. Your location is always the same/Notice how you alter your sense of location by shifting the focus of attention.

All location is relative to position. Distance is relative to location.

Focus of attention: Sensory-perceptive
                               Sensation
 Valence + or -   Thought
  Ambivalence   Feeling

Identity

Knowing- created informational system.

Meaning—Changes from your position/Identity/storyline

Process—how you reach a particular orientation

Predicting- use of the created information system across time/events.

Controlling- regulation of outcomes based on knowing and predicting.

Fusion- Merging with thoughts feelings, observation

Con-fusion- self forgetting when merging and then self-forgetting

Yoga and the Consciousness

Whether you are doing meditation, yoga, cognitive behavior therapy or any form of self management, you will need to focus, concentrate and direct the attention. Actually, I find awareness of the focus of attention is helpful in clearing the consciousness. Dharana is concentration and then there is karma yoga or focus on action, Bhakti yoga or focus on devotion and Ghan yoga or focus on knowledge. Yoga is the yoking or containing and directing the energy of the mind/body or consciousness. In tantra yoga or study there is the pursuit of the divine through focused energy. In *Kabbalah* or Hebrew mysticism the focusing of the energy is through the *Sefirot* or energetic containers. At the crown is the light/ *Kether* or will which moves toward force /wisdom or undifferentiated energy then moves toward understanding/ or form which is differentiated energy and then the merging of these two is *knowledge* which is an air element which moves toward mercy/love which is expansive energy which is moved toward judgment/severity or contraction of energy and with the merging of these two energies in beauty which is a fluid element. These energies move toward eternity/cycles and reverberation which is reflection and concludes or resolves in the foundation or earth and Kingdom. The Ain which is Nothing becomes Ayin Sof or Absolute Nothing and is pierced or energized by the Ayin sof Aur or the Infinite Light. The universe said to be born in and through light and sound.

The example below is a representation of the Tree of Life and the movement of the light and sound or energy.

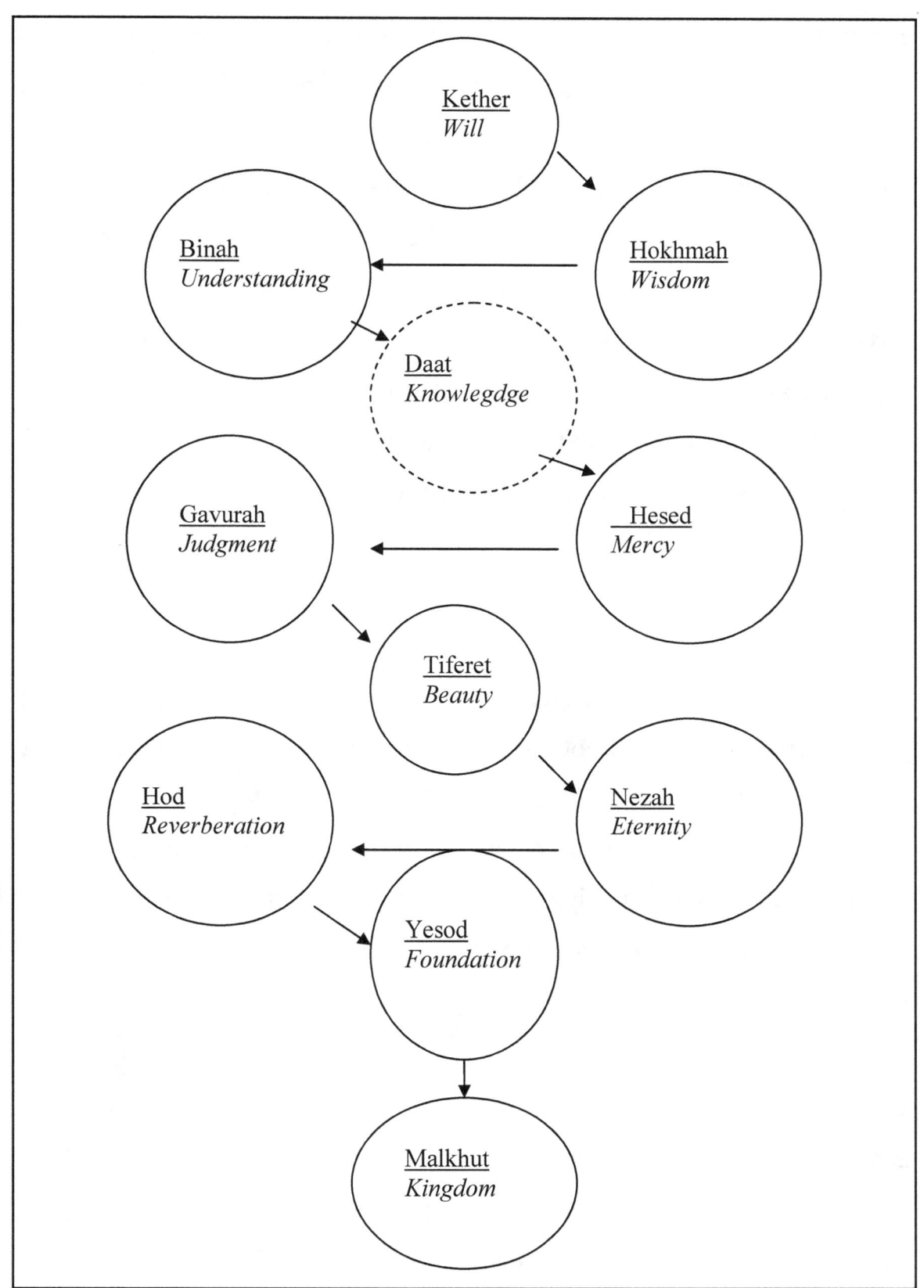

TREE OF LIFE

The yoga or yoking of awareness with the consciousness is moving from the clouds to the sky the infinite expanse that contains both and neither. Stephen Wolinsky suggests that Sri Nisargadatta Maharaj talks of the non-verbal I am/ the verbal I am and beyond. One step is I am nothing, the next step is I am everything the third step is the non-dual self or there is neither I am or I am not. No me. No you. The Buddhist teaching of: it is neither this, nor that, not both, nor neither. Whatever you say it is, it is not. In this particular awareness training, we are noticing the unpacking or loosening of concepts and frameworks so that one is at home moving in and through the frameworks and lenses that have been overlaid on the absolute. The absolute is that which is and isn't, is both and neither. It is neither perceivable nor conceivable.

> The exercise is to become aware of the lens, be the lens, pretend you are not the lens and that you did not create it, that the lens has always been there, have amnesia for the lens and its origin. Let the concept/ lens be foreground, let it be background, stand or be aware of being between the foreground and background but being neither ,now be the space that contains both, but is neither. Now, turn the attention around and ask what knower knows that, and what if anything created all of that?

The teaching that you use a concept to loosen, remove, dislodge or change another concept and then give them both up applies. Things are only true as long as they are and things are only false as long as they are and the temporary nature of things, concepts and ideas tells us that they are appearances and are not. Don't sweat the small stuff, it's all small stuff. The "Great Way" is easy unless you have preferences. Straight is the gate and narrow is the way and few there be that find it. Noticing the blissful Essence of the absolute takes time to stabilize because the soul is willing but the form is weak and gets distracted by the illusion or Maya. We are working on becoming a more productive, healthier, happier illusion. As Maharaj stated "You are the child of a barren woman.", and we are now constructing your wardrobe and the drama for a hundred lifetimes." The lies and stories we tell ourselves and each other are the echoes of emptiness in a canyon that has no walls. The exercise is about contextualizing, re-contextualizing and de-contextualizing the awareness of the concepts grounding the body /mind to present time sensory alignment and re-emerging not as to be more true or better but as a way of loosening the samskaras/ impressions and mind tendencies and attachments to those impressions and solidifying them into a pattern.

Absolute

Quantum

Sub Atomic

Chemical

Elemental

Organic

(Homeostasis)

Neural Information Centers

Unarticulated Programming (Non-Verbal)

Made up of (Neuro-Transmitters, Neuro-Peptides Electro-chemical interactions)

These have upward and downward mobility and parallel processing

Convergent

And Divergent

Emergent

Synthesis

Development of Associational Pathways

Visual   Auditory   Tactile   Olfactory   Gustatory   Kinesthetic

"Context"   Position   Distance

Time reference

Background/foreground "Mirror of Existence"

Just Noticeable Difference

Recognition/ Information—Mis-information /Programming Errors

Meaning "Knowledge"

Errors in Meaning and Perception

Frame-Reframe-De-Frame

Alteration in Processing

Sensory Perceptive Alteration

Sensory Perceptive Holographic Interactive Mapping System

"Homeostasis"

Gestalt/Expansion   Homeostasis/Contraction

Prediction/Control

Judgment/ Preference/ Significance and No JPS

Meta view ....Micro-View

False conclusion/False solution

Diamond of Awareness

Life on Life's Terms

Beyond

All stories are stories and are meant for the ignorant to occupy the mind, and give them something to talk about. See beyond the illusion.

Be beyond the illusion.

You are not what you take yourself to be.

Techniques must be used and then given up.

You cannot realize with a technique or teaching.

A man came to Maharaj and asked, "Master, Don't I deserve peace?" Maharaj answered, "Those who deserve peace do not disturb it".

It is best that we each discover for ourselves how, when, and if a particular teaching applies in our life. For me this teaching meant that I cannot stop or control the storms and disturbances created by others, however, I do not have to throw rocks and cause more turmoil in the calm waters of the lake in my world.

Sensory-Perceptive Identification Alignment

As you begin to notice your identities and the way you perceive the world and have experiences, one of the most useful tools is the use of observational skills. These observational skills employ the use of visual, auditory, tactile, kinesthetic, gustatory, and olfactory notation. In this time, and with our present state of brain research we have also become aware of the possible utilization of mirror neurons as a means to infer the internal states of those we seek to observe. An essential question is through what eyes, ears, skin, feelings, and meanings will one seek to observe. We experience the universe through the internal mapping system that is an abstracted representation of the universe that has been developed and created through and by the interpretations of the individual and others.

Neuro Linguistic Programming is a particular way of interpreting human perception and it discusses three (3) primary positions for observation: position one is the self-position, position two (2) is the observer position while position three (3) is the other position. Each of these positions can be considered multiple, for there are numerous variations within each position.

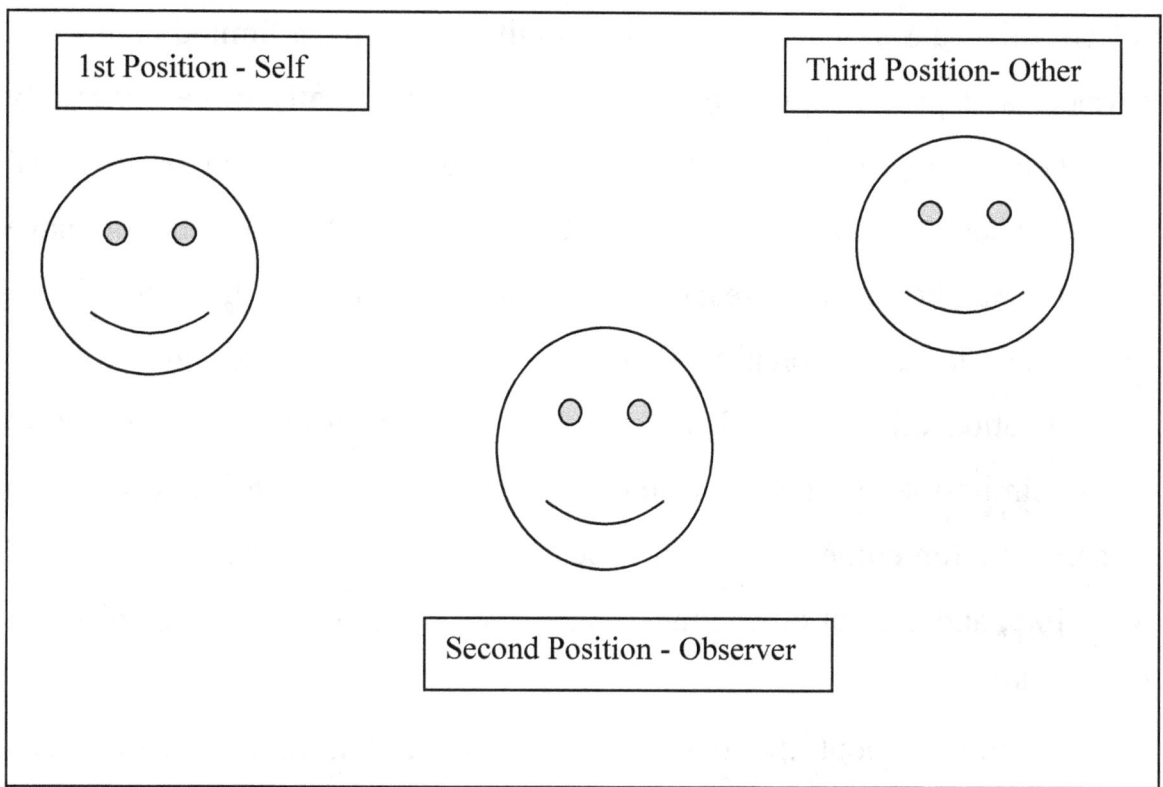

As we begin to have observation occur, one grounding position is to seek present time sensory alignment and move toward no judgment, no preference, no significance, and no references. As Stephen Wolinsky, Ph.D. would say "no frames of reference, no references to frame" or at the very least becoming aware of these lenses as a source conceptual filtering. Keep in mind that often these can happen unknowingly, unconsciously and unintentionally, so reverse the way that it happens so that it is done knowingly, consciously and intentionally. Remember that Identities are created positions in space-time. In addition, our world interpretation is no more accurate or real than the maps, representations and interpretations of others.

G.I Gurdjieff a *Sufi* teacher stated that individuals have a limited number of physical and psychological postures. Identities are really more accurately described as a probability function in that they arise when needed and subside when the stimulus is gone. As Gurdjieff indicated we generally have a limited number of these responses, so it may appear that the person has a somewhat stable personality. This probably has more to do with the generalization effect, as well as other hypnotic distortions that help us to merge similarities so that it would appear that the person has a constant personality. Sometimes the person's behavior seems to be more transient and wave like, and then at other times it appears to be more solid like an object or particle.

When thinking about the observer keep mind, that in fact there is no observer, it is a created position that appears when there is observation. Turn your attention around and ask, *"What observer ask and answers the question? What observer observes that, and what if anything did all of that."*

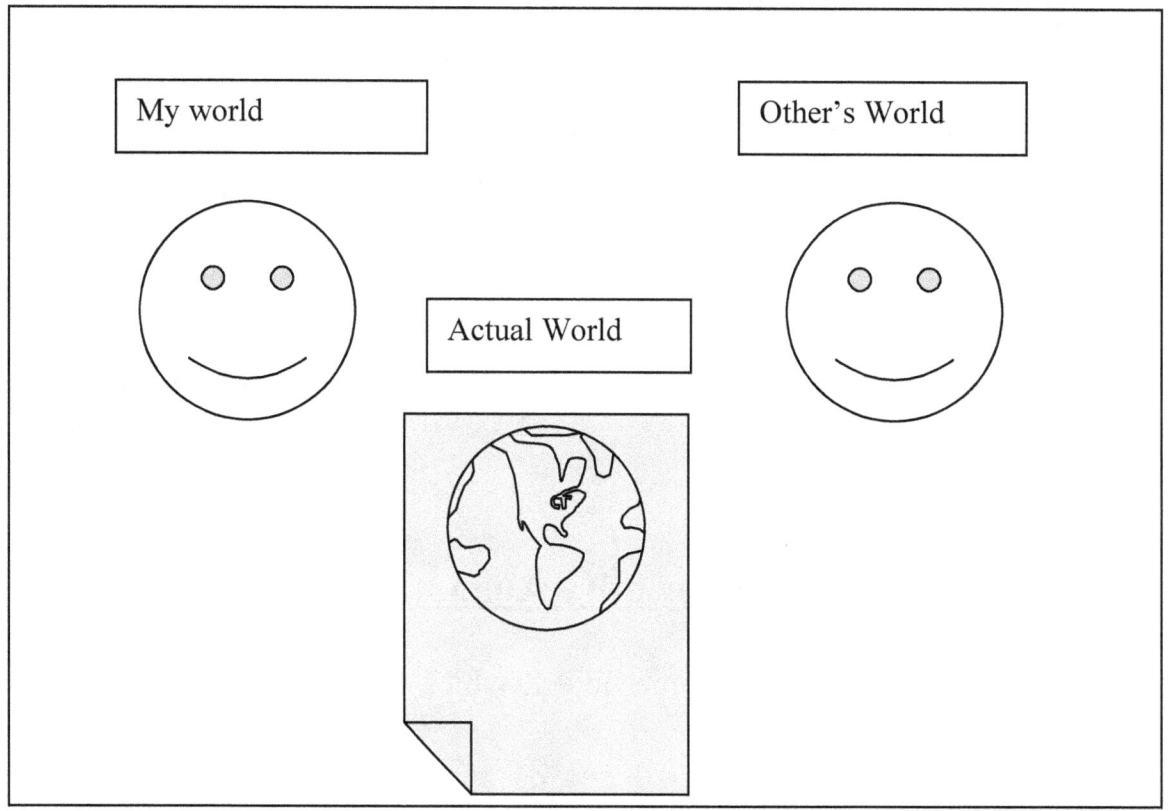

We need to keep in mind that each of us lives in the world, but experiences the world through the sensory perceptive interactive holographic mapping system. Each individual is born as an essential energetic being. The organism or biological being has certain needs that must be met for the being to survive. Socialization is the imposition of the familial, tribal, and cultural rules and interpretations of how, when, where, if and in what manner to meet those needs. One schism created in the development of self is the division of the biological and the social person or as Maharaj taught, the being-ness and the conceptual person and its life.

The first loss of the organism is of the self. We give up our person/self in order to get something from others, such as parents or people in charge. The things we seek can be material such as food, shelter clothing, etc. or the things we may seek could be less tangible like love, approval, affection, recognition or some other emotional or conceptual need.

Each of the observation positions is a created position. We recommend that you first seek Present Time Sensory Alignment. Follow the listed instructions:

There is only one question, and that question is *"Who or what do you Imagine or pretend that you are?" There are a million variations, aspects, or clarifications to this question.*

Present Time Sensory Perceptive Alignment:

Step 1. Begin by gazing at some object, which has neutral association for you.

Step 2. Sit or lie comfortably.

Step 3. Describe to yourself what it feels likes to position yourself in the seat, chair, or bed. For example, I can feel my entire body sinking into the fabric of the chair. I can feel my left foot (sensing) it feels heavier than my right foot. My muscles are beginning to feel limp. My breathing is beginning to slow and is now deeper in my chest.

Step 4. Take three deeper than normal breaths – slow, deep breaths, and upon each breath think to yourself R-E-L-A-X, allowing the air to slowly, leak out with each exhalation.

Step 5. You can allow your eyes to close. However, you can be in a deep comfortable state with your eyes open or closed.

Self-Pacing

Step 6. Try to hear and become aware of as many elements (sounds) in the environment as possible.

Step 7. Allow the sounds to be linked by the centers with images. Allow any images to be linked with the sounds. Allow any thoughts of the past or the future to be redirected back to the present streaming of thoughts.

Step 8. Now allow your thoughts to be projected onto a screen that you visualize out in front of you, about ten feet away and slightly above eye level. The screen becomes the channel through which and by which thoughts are conducted. Sound thoughts are even heard as running through the screen display.

Step 9. Now give your *neural information centers* permission to operate independently performing the following:

    (a) Redirect all thought to the present time (no past or... future thoughts).

        (I) Start one center counting down from 1000 to 0 by 1's.

        (II) Start another center counting from one to 1000.

        (III) Have another center send commands to the body to "be calm – relax".

        (IV) Have yet another center narrate and create a healthy body state.

Step 10. Remind yourself if you start feeling overwhelmed to let go and allow the centers to do their work. A center can check in from time to time on its status, but let them do their work. Trust the centers.

Step 11. Continue to allow the centers to develop their autonomy.

Step 12. Recognize any source of tension in the body and request that the center in charge provide "release and relaxation".

Step 13. Allow the steps above to become a more fluid and flexible schema under the direction of the h*omeostatic* system, rather than a rigid schema. Remember the *homeostatic* system is seeking balance and congruency. *Sometimes, homeostasis may present itself by resisting change. In its search for balance and trying to preserve sameness, homeostasis may generate anxiety or trepidation concerning the change.*

Step 14. Count from one to five when signaled by a *neural information center* to do so. Allow your eyes to open, and be fully alert and present.

Relax

After you have reached a state of *Present Time Sensory Alignment*, you may also be interested in experiencing a taste of the *essential self*. The internal nature of self is the *ineffable, the indescribable* or it may be perceived as void or nothingness, and with that label and misinformation it is experienced as negative or bad. Therefore, we turn our focus outward seeking fulfillment and completion outside of the self. As Dr. Stephen Wolinsky stated we are seeking "Love in all the wrong places." Prior to all conceptions is the essential space, labeling the space means it is not, THAT. Working on the Essential self one encounters the layers of concepts that have been abstracted over the absolute.

Non-Verbal I AM (Beingness)

Verbal I AM (I AM +)

Logos (Source of Causality)

Philosophy

Belief Systems

Strategies

Beliefs

Concepts

Ideas

Thoughts

Feelings

Emotions

Animal

Vegetable

Mineral

Chemical

Atomic

Sub-Atomic

As you discover the essence of the self, you may discover the levels of conceptualization created by the consciousness and the socialization process.

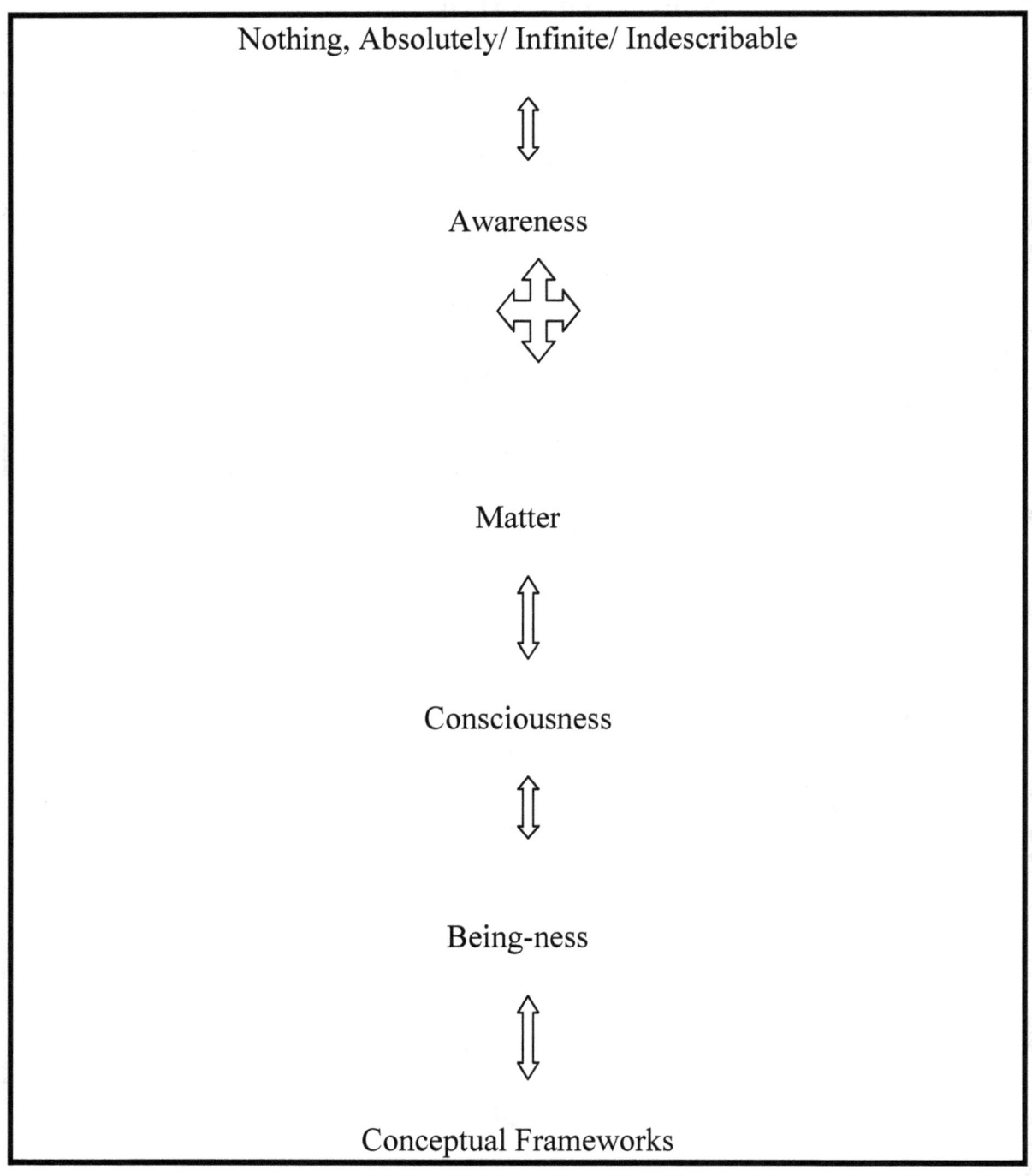

As the *void* or *spaciousness*, which, felt internally is misperceived as a lack, the loss of self creates the false core and the false-self compensator. They come in pairs. False conclusions invariably lead to false solutions.

False Core	False Core Compensator
1. There must be something Wrong with me.	1. Prove there is nothing wrong with me. By acting Perfect
2. I am Worthless	2. Prove I am worthy. By acting like I have Worth or Value.
3. I cannot Do, act or decide.	3. Prove that I can do. By acting like I an Over-Achiever.
4. I am Inadequate	4. Prove that I am not inadequate. By acting Over Adequate and smart.
5. I do not Exist, I am Nothing, I have Nothing.	5. Prove that I do exist. By acting as if I do Exist or Am something.
6. I am Alone	6. Prove or act as if I am Connected.
7. I am Incomplete, there must be Something Missing, I am not Enough.	7. Prove that I am Not incomplete, or act as if I feel complete.
8. I am Powerless	8. Prove I am not Powerless and act as if I am powerful.
9. I am Loveless, there is no Love.	9. Prove I am not Loveless and act as if I am Lovable and loving.

These are the distortions of the "I" and Stephen Wolinsky stated that there were 5 strategies that the individual generally uses for dealing with the false self. The **5 R**s are re-enacting, re-sisting, re-creating, re-solving and re-enforcing. Three things to be aware of about this false core are: *1*. The first created identity is the strongest. 2. The I am precedes the false-core. Remember, "Tell me a difference between you and the false-core, you and this thought, you and this feeling, etc." *3*. This "I" you call you is part of the complex. As Maharaj said, "Which came first you or this "I"?" Also consider, What Observer, observes all of this? Fixating on any of these points of conceptualization distracts us from the *"truth"* which is that we do not know how or why things occur. The nervous system is more comfortable creating *Knowledge* so that it can pretend to *know*, because if we know then we can *predict* what will occur. By *predicting* we believe or tell ourselves that we can *control* the outcome.

When we mistakenly look inside and feel the **spaciousness** which is mislabeled as *emptiness*, the tendency is to focus our attention outwardly into the world of people, places and things, where we begin looking for our meaning, hope and strength in the imaginary objects in our perceived world. The particular interpretation of the lack is what Stephen Wolinsky called the false core. He took the 9 fixation points of the Enneagram as one way of describing the nervous system's interpretation of this imagined flaw. The *Gestalt* process of the developing mind needing to *know, predict* and *control* creates a reason why the person failed to achieve the goal or didn't get some perceived desire. The actual reason things occur or don't occur is because they do or don't occur. The false self is the counter-point to the false core. If I perceive that the cause of my loss is my *imperfection* then surely the remedy is to become more *perfec*t. The fusion-confusion-illusion is that by creating a false cause I now begin the struggle and cycle of attempting to correct something that is a lie. You cannot solve something that is not true. **_False conclusions lead to false solutions_**. The essential step of awareness is to realize that the false core-false self dyad is two halves of the mirrored reflection where each creates the other, they are not separate. As has been said by numerous wise teachers "happiness is an inside job" or as Milton Erickson stated "the answer is within." Causality is an illusion and a game that the nervous system plays pretending that if it can know, then it can create a different outcome. As Jim Morrison once said, "No one gets out of here alive."

<u>Loss of Essence</u>

One of the first casualties of the socialization process is the dimming or loss of awareness of the essential space and along with that what we call essential qualities of the person. The inner spaciousness of the person is the remnant of the infinite or the void. That which is the absolute, the indefinable, which is beyond description, is what we are made up of. The symbol of a burning candle is a metaphor that demonstrates, the body like the wax is made of elements that are slowly consumed as the flame illuminates the surrounding area. The wick like the nervous system connects the elements of the body with the elements of the air, and as the spark ignites the process of the flame which is neither the inert elements of the candle nor the unseen elements of the air. The flame like consciousness produces light and heat which are evidence of the aliveness of the flame but these are just by products of the process the fire. The phenomena of the flame can be seen, felt, heard and experienced but they are not actually there, for at each moment they are in the process of becoming something else. The flame is neither this nor that, nor neither nor both. The example of the flame of the candle is an example of the transmutation of elements. The combustive awakening of the candle into heat and light gives it the appearance of a dancer in the night casting shadows on the landscape. Such is the nature of consciousness where its effects are seen but where is the consciousness.

As the individual develops there is an interactive, phenomenal process whereby the persona is created. As the individual develops physiologically, neurologically and sociologically the organism goes through stages of dependency upon the caregivers. The levels of dependency are symbiotic/dependent, counter-dependent, independent and then inter-dependent. Throughout the organism's life there will be changes and alterations in the levels of need dependency required. There are any number of theoretical proposals for the Neuro/psycho/physiological development of the individual. The limbic system is the first to go on line and ensure the survival of the physical being. As the conceptual or social person begins to develop the generational/familial/cultural influence has its impact upon the developing neural information centers. Neural information centers are the symbolic representation Dr. Hellams and Mr. Schreiber have chosen to label this interactive process of the neurological process of information and association creation and strengthening.

The particular refraction of the energetic flow through the individual energy field is interpreted in a particular way. The Enneagram describes 9 interactive points of fixation the points are:

Perfection

Worth

Doing

Adequacy

Existence

Connection

Complete

Power

Love

The variations and movements of the triads are thinking, feeling and acting/relating, another triad is Self-forgetting, Image Creation and Paranoia. Another triad is Anger, What Am I Feeling? , and the Fear.

Action

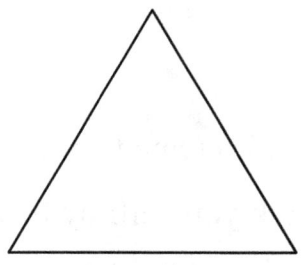

Thinking　　　　Feeling

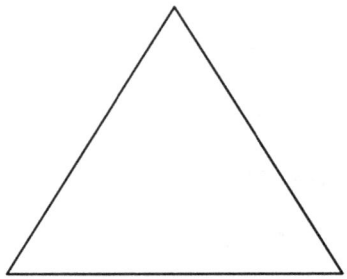

Self-Forgetting

Paranoia   Image creation

Movement within consciousness is just an alternation in focus. Remember forgetting who you are leads to image creation and since the image is false this leads to paranoia or fear.

Identities have functions:

When an identity is created it is created with a function in mind or as a strategy to get something. Ask yourself; by being that what am I seeking, wanting, needing, resisting or avoiding? If that doesn't occur what will be the worst of it? If it does happen what gets created, not created or resisted? By imagining that you need to change or become different than you are, what lie do you need to tell yourself?

When you develop a strategy ask yourself:

How is that working?	**What are you resisting?**
What are you getting?	**What are you avoiding?**
What are you being?	**What are you not getting?**
What are you doing?	**What are you not being?**
What are you wanting?	**What are you not having?**
What are you needing?	**What are you not doing?**
What are you wishing for?	**What are you not creating?**
What are you hoping for?	**What are you not making?**
What are you imagining?	
What are creating?	
What are you making?	

Questions help us to sort out what is occurring inside the mapping system. It assists us in noticing the strategy, belief or concept that underlies the particular action, belief or framework.

If you get that, what then?
If that occurs, what will it be?
If that occurs, what won't it be?
It that does not occur, what then?

> **If that does not occur, what won't it be?**
>
> **What will it mean?**
>
> **What won't it mean?**
>
> **When that happens what will it be?**
>
> **When that happens what won't it be?**
>
> **When that doesn't happen what will occur?**
>
> **As that happens what will it be.?**

Relationships fail because we lie to ourselves about ourselves, our motives, or about the other person.

As Dr. Wolinsky suggested, "What did you, assume, decide or believe that got you to creating or doing that. The false core gets created because we realize that we are alone or, decide that something did or did not happen for us, then we create that this occurred because of some missing characteristic. We the further decide if we can get or create that characteristic or quality, we will be whole, reconnected, or reach nirvana/heaven. In reality, things either occur or things do not occur, but we create a story to explain the event and tell ourselves, if we do what we need to, then we will get what we want. Infantile grandiosity and magical thinking are fueled by the Gestalt process of completion.

Notice, how we look into the perceived emptiness and feel a lack, then look out into the world searching for fulfillment and completion. What we seek was never missing and we are looking outside of ourselves when the answer is within.

The "I AM" is the source of all the stories and experiences. Who or what do you imagine that you are? Remember even space and time are imagined. One of the ways that Dr. Wolinsky suggested to work with the *False* core is to create it, to experience it and to, then un-create it. To be free from something you must be free to have it and free not to have it.

Exercise:

Discovering the false core.
1. If something does not happen for you, what is the worst of it?
2. If I do not get that promotion, relationship or job it will just prove "I am worthless." If my mother does not love me, I am no good.
3. Is that the worst of it? No, if I am worthless then I will be alone.
4. And if you are alone, what's the worst of that?
5. I won't exist. I am nothing. Yes, that is it the nothingness.

Processing the False Core-False Self

Step 1. Become aware of your false core

Step 2. Notice the emptiness and create your False core.

Step 3. Notice a difference between you and your false Core.

Step 4. Notice the size and shape of the false core. (This is enhanced by stepping out of the false core, to observe).

Step 5. Now, take a moment to notice all the different associational links and networks that are attached to the *False core*. If your False Core is "I am Imperfect", notice the associations connected and stemming from and to it. This is the core of your psychology and it pushes you to solve it.

Step 6. Become aware of the energy and attention tied up in the core dyad.

Step 7. Notice how the core pulls your attention to it.

Step 8. Now, notice how if you expand your awareness to allow it there is awareness of the Big Emptiness the core is floating in.

Step 9. Ask the false core (allow it to answer) what it is seeking more than anything in the world?

Step 10. When you get a sense of what it is seeking, ask yourself, "And if I felt that Essential quality, what would that feel like?" Be it peace, love, strength, etc.

Step 11. Now step into your Essential Core and notice how it feels.

Step 12. From the Essential core and with the Essential quality notice the False Core and it's associations with all their intensity, floating in the Big Emptiness.

Step 13. Now, have them turn and notice that what they have been seeking is and has always been in Essence.

Step 14. Take the label off of the False Core and have it as Energy.

Step 15. Now, notice that the False Core and the Big Emptiness are made of the same substance. Notice what happens.

Step 16. Continue to experience the Essential Core and the Essential quality as you split your awareness in 3 ways. 1/3 on the Essential Core, 1/3 on whatever may arise and 1/3 on the room as awareness returns to here and now.

Step 17. Now, notice as you turn your attention around, what observer observes that. What if anything created all of that?

Breathe and be here!

ESSENCE AND THE THERAPY OF PRESENCE

It is difficult to define essence, that which is essential. The essence of the person is the infinite and indescribable. Whatever you can say about it, it is not. Essence has been called by other names (energy, chit, awareness, undifferentiated consciousness, spirit, etc.) These are the labels and names given to Essence. The body/mind forms around the essence, which is the empty space we experience/feel when we look within. As the consciousness observes the world of people, places and things, it also becomes aware that these objects appear and disappear. This observation creates chaos, confusion, not knowing and a feeling of being out of control. As this consciousness becomes aware of its own disappearance it feels fear. This fear becomes fused/ attached to all of the creations of consciousness, such as: {*thoughts, feelings, sensations, emotions, beliefs, philosophies, expectations, stories, lessons, associations, observers, identities, energy, mass and space- time, etc.*}

The Diamond of Awareness

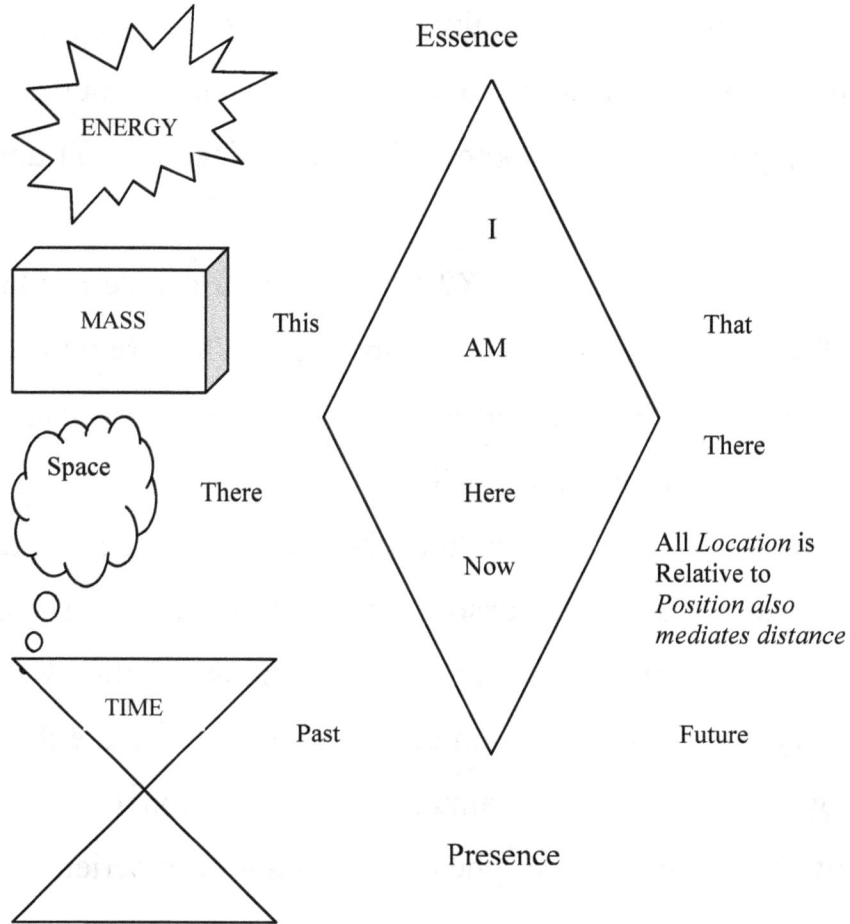

Looking within itself the consciousness sees spaciousness/Essence, and labels it as emptiness and weakness. Then consciousness looks outside of itself into the world of people, places and things which it perceives as transient, appearing and disappearing. This

Fear of disappearance drives a need to know to prevent the disappearance. The nervous system creates a structure over itself and its world in order to define it, create order and have knowledge.

This structure is the *Sensory Perceptive Holographic Interactive Mapping System*/function. The function of the nervous system is to survive and the function of the map is to enhance survival by *knowing, predicting,* and *controlling.* The nervous system organizes the universe into what it wants to know and what it does not want to know. We can ask ourselves the questions: What are you willing to know about X? What are you unwilling to know about X?

What did you decide to know about X? What did you decide not to know about X? What are you resisting knowing about X? What are you resisting not knowing about X? What are you withholding from yourself about X? What lies are you telling yourself about X?

This experience is sometimes referred to as the conscious/unconscious split. The way of homeostasis is to alter sensory information to maintain sameness with our sensing of stimuli and our representations of the world and ourselves. Sensory perceptive alteration or trance phenomena are the results of this effort by the organism to maintain its organizational integrity and structure. Following are the types of phenomena you may experience.

TRANCE PHENOMENA

"Feelings are interactive perceptions."
Antonio Damasio

One of the primary ways bio-psycho-*homeostasis* is maintained is through the mechanism of *sensory perceptive alteration (SPA)*. This phenomenon is involved in the realignment and construction of the sensorial mapping world. It is one of the mechanisms in the editing of the experiential world. The human organism has the ability to alter sensory data so that it will conform to the preexisting neural information pool contained in the *sensory perceptive holographic mapping.* Several elements appear common to *sensory perceptive alteration*:

A. There appears to be a narrowing, shrinking, or fixating of attention. This change in attention is experienced as happening to the person.

B. There is a spontaneous emergence of other *sensory perceptive alteration*s (<u>Trances People Live</u>, Wolinsky, Stephen 1991). The interweaving of altered, Sensory Perceptive data is one of the keys to the confabulatory nature of the *sensory perceptive holographic mapping*.

C. The alterations influence the experience of energy, space, mass, and time.

D. The effect of *sensory perceptive alteration* is the editing of sensory data by deletions, distortions, generalizations, additions, confabulations, and changes within associational meaning.

E. There is a beginning, middle, and end of the phenomena, although the *trance* continuum never ends.

F. There is an appearance of a "conscious" and other conscious split. Frequently there is the sense of a split between reality and *trance*.

There is always ongoing, *sensory perceptive alteration* for the nervous system continuously organizes the sensory flow and creates the experience of a knowable, predictable world. Often when a sensory alteration occurs, it is accompanied by other alterations of sensory perception or interpretation. The following are the different types of *sensory perceptive alteration*s that have been observed and named:

1. *Age Regression:*

Age regression is a distinct feeling in which the person feels younger than his chronological age or experiences being at an earlier time in his life. Auditory, visual, kinesthetic, or other types of hallucinations, as well as sensory or time distortion often accompany this *sensory perceptive alteration*.

Examples:
A. Bill remembers a time he was called into his boss's office, and before he ever arrived there, he had begun to imagine what kind of trouble he might be in. As the pictures and images flashed in front of him, he heard his boss's voice, and it sounded like his father's voice the

time he was grounded in the 4th grade. The voice sounded deep and booming, and he felt small and childlike, like he did when he was younger. He stated that he often feels like this when he is being confronted about difficulties, even if he has done nothing wrong

B. Susan, now in her fifties, described feeling as giddy as a high schooler while on a beach trip with her friends, as they laughed and talked about memories of beach trips they had shared when they were in high school.

Examples from your experience:
(1)
_____

_____

(2)
_____

_____

2. *Age Progression or Pseudo Orientation in Time:*

Age progression or pseudo orientation in time is often used to designate future thoughts and images but could also refer to neutral or undesignated points in time.

Examples:
A. Robert stated that as the meeting for his promotion approached, he became concerned and began to anticipate the results. He could see images of himself and the committee as they inform him of the reasons he was not going to receive an upgrade, even though he knew he had worked hard and had earned the promotion.

B. Julie, thinking about her wedding day, which is only two months away, describes hearing herself saying her vows to Tom, and hearing Tom saying his vows to her. Her thoughts feel so real, she sometimes cries tears of joy.

C. Andrew meditates for peace and stress relief. He states that one of the benefits of this focused relaxation is a sense of there being the absence of time.

Examples from your experience:

(1)

---

(2)

---

3. *Dissociation:*

Dissociation is a blocking of the ability to experience internal feelings or sensations, external body parts or external events or things.

Examples:

A: Joe and Elizabeth have pet names for their sexual organs and talk about her "monkey" and his "banana." As in this illustration, names are given to body parts as if they are separate from the person.

B: Jerry states that he feels angry most of the time, but does not ever remember a feeling of sadness. He says these types of feelings were not expressed in his family, and he does not remember his father ever expressing sadness. In fact, his father said, "the Williams men never show sadness, and it is a sign of weakness if you do."

C: Angie remembers her mother saying that her father had a problem with alcohol; however, she has no memory of her father's drunken rages or the abuse he acted out on the family.

Examples from your experience:
(1)

_____

_____

(2)

_____

_____

4. *Post-Hypnotic Suggestion:*

Interpersonal communication or interaction that is internalized and becomes an intrapersonal communication self to self in the form of introjects or auditory dialogues.

Examples:
A. Rodney is very successful at his job as a computer-programming consultant. He can still hear his father telling him that you have to get up early and work hard to be a success. He finds it difficult to relax and slow down, even though there is no concern about his business being successful.

B. Kelly has difficulty being assertive, even though she is a trained counselor. She remembers her mother's words that polite people and ladies don't talk back, but they do what they're told.

C. In the movie "What the Bleep, Do We Know" the Native Americans were unable to see the explorers' ships until given the programming by the Shaman of whom they implicitly trusted. (What the Bleep, Do We Know, 2004)

Examples from your experience:
(1)

_____

_____

(2)

5. *Amnesia, Denial, Hypermnesia:*

The continuum of remembering and forgetting, that is critical to the creation and maintenance of the *sensory perceptive holographic map*. Forgetting things; pushing thoughts, feelings, or memories down; or over-remembering are all on the continuum of memory.

   Examples:
   A.   Paul pushes back the feeling that his drinking has gotten out of control or that his problem remembering the night's events is not disturbing to him. He tells everyone that everything is fine and he is doing well, but that is not the truth.

   B. Amber and her husband Michael are seeing a marital counselor for conflict in their relationship. Michael cannot seem to remember what happens in their arguments, while Amber remembers everything in painfully vivid details, much to his embarrassment.

Examples from your experience:
(1)

(2)

6. *Negative Hallucinations:*

A negative hallucination is a complex internal *trance* process that edits out one's internal experience of perception. When experiencing a negative hallucination, a person does not see what is seen by others, or hear what is heard by others, or feel what is felt by others, or taste what others taste, or smell what others can smell.

Examples:
A. How many times can you remember looking for your car or house keys, only to discover that they were right in front of you the entire time? Think of the times you were deeply engrossed in a good book, watching a fantastic movie, or really enjoying a close ball game and suddenly became aware that someone had been calling you for several minutes, and you had not heard the first sound. Objects, sounds, textures, and many other stimuli from every area of the senses are at times out of one's awareness are somehow altered or removed from the sensory mapping.

Examples:
B. Laura talks about the time she was concentrating on her artwork and did not hear her daughter calling her because the soup was boiling over and the dinner was nearly ruined.

C. In the movie "What the Bleep, Do We Know," the Native Americans could not see Columbus's ships because they had no previous frame of reference through which to interpret the new stimuli. (What the Bleep, Do We Know, 2004)

Examples from your experience:
(1)

_____

_____

(2)

_____

_____

7. *Positive Hallucination:*

A positive hallucination, like its opposite twin, the negative hallucination alters one's perception of the experiential world. With the a positive hallucination, a person can hear, see, feel, smell, or taste what is not there. Positive and negative hallucinations are part of the editing function of the organism as they assist in the adding and the subtracting of the sensory stimuli and perception of those stimuli in the creation and synthesis of the *sensory perceptive holographic mapping.*

Positive hallucinations can be simple or complex and like other *sensory perceptive alteration*s will work in concert with other alterations. These hallucinations are often observed with completion errors where the organism is filling in, subtracting, or distorting sensory perception to keep harmony in the mapping process. The need of the organism to have or create closure may be a driving force behind these alterations. Some types of hallucinations are state or context dependent and only occur when specific emotions or events are present.

> A. When Jennifer ask Monte if he wants to go to lunch, he hears her saying she's interested in a relationship with him.

> B. A child's imaginary friend is a type of positive hallucination, such as John has a friend, "Mr. Elf" whom he plays with for hours when no other playmates are available. This is often context dependent as it goes away when other people arrive. Some types of phenomena are state dependent and occur when specific emotional states are present.

Examples from your experience:
(1)

_____

_____

(2)

_____

_____

8. Confusion:

Confusion is a sensory alteration that can occur when an individual experiences being overwhelmed, threatened by new information or unfamiliar sensory stimuli. This includes role confusion, task confusion or self-generated confusion. The following are examples of each type of confusion.

Examples:
A. Self- generated confusion:
Tyler, usually a quiet and reserved young man, becomes quite agitated, creating much yelling and screaming in the house, when he notices the argument between his parents. His behavior escalates to the point that the parents have to stop what they are doing in order to stop the confusion created by his behavior.

B. Task Confusion:
Susan, an accomplished pianist, turns to her husband Billy and says, "I can't program this VCR. You know I never could do any type of technical things, and my father always told me to stay away from electronic objects."

C. Role Confusion:
Freud, who coined the "Whore-Madonna Syndrome," identifies confusion as a "syndrome." This case involved an individual who enjoyed having a sexual relationship with a performer whom he perceived as being promiscuous, only to marry her and then find after

the marriage, he had transferred all the feelings he had toward his mother to her, and had absolutely no sexual desire for her.

Examples from your experience:
(1)

(2)

9. *Time Distortion:*

Time distortion is an alteration in the perception and interpretation of time. There are several things to notice about time; the individual creates an experience of time in his body. The individual sustains the experience of time by putting it on automatic and the individual can subjectively alter how he experiences the sense of time he has created. Milton H. Erickson is reported to have said "time" is a construct. Time can be perceived as moving at different rates of speed. Have you ever felt like time just disappears or that it just seems to drag. Individuals describe that they experience themselves as going through time or are in time. Time is treated as if it were an object; however, time is a fluid concept.

Examples:
A. David's girlfriend insists that they go to a movie he designates as a "chick flick." As David sits there, he munches his popcorn, attempting to make the time go. He continually reminds himself how bad the experience is and how the time just seems to drag. For David, instead of two hours, the movie seems to last ten.

B. Sally, on her way to work, is involved in an automobile accident. As she is going through the intersection, someone runs the red light. They tap the end of her car, sending it into a spin. Sally feels as though the whole world has gone into slow motion. She experiences, a sense of spinning, a sense of trying to control the steering wheel, and a sense of trying to grapple for control of the brake. She reports after the car finally stops, "It seemed like an eternity before the car would stop."

Examples from your experience:
(1)

(2)

10. *Hypnotic Dreaming:*

Hypnotic dreaming takes the place of healthy action toward realization of a plan or goal. It often takes place automatically without the person's conscious direction.

Example:
A. Jackie dreams about being a motion picture star. However, Jackie has never been in one play. She has never answered any of the advertisements with a local college to work as an extra in any of their plays. She has refused the offers of friends to be involved as an extra on a film being shot nearby. She spends hours thinking each day in a fantasy world, about the mansion she will live in, the limousine she will ride in, and the rewards she will receive as a star.

Examples from your experience:
(1)

(2)

11. *Sensory Distortion:*

Sensory distortion is an alteration of the sensed stimuli at variance with what the individual may normally experience. There are three types of sensory distortion: These are psycho-physiological sensory distortion in which unwanted sensations are numbed, dulled, or overly intensified; hyper-or hypo- sensory distortion in which environmental stimuli are amplified or obliterated; and pain sensory distortion in which only the afflicted portion of the body is perceived.

Examples:

A: George, while talking with his therapist, begins to notice the ticking of the clock. The noise becomes more and more irritating as he tries to think about what he is discussing with his therapist, to the point he almost feels as if he will scream, the ticking of the clock is so disturbing to him.

B. Jane plans to attend a formal event that is very important to her. The day prior to the event, she notices a slight pimple near her left cheek. As the event approaches, she sees the pimple becoming larger, redder, pulsating more, throbbing more, and becoming monumental in terms of her face. Instead of a slight imperfection, she sees it as almost covering half her face.

C. After Carol, a pain patient, leaves the room, the physician remarks to the nurse "given the injury and procedures she has received, there is just no structural or physiological reason why she is experiencing so much pain in her lumbar region."

Examples from your experience:

(1)

_____

_____

(2)

_____

_____

Cluster Trances: (The next two *sensory perceptive alteration* states are what we consider cluster *trance*s because they actually utilize and incorporate several different *trance* states to accomplish their effect.)

12. Gestalt Closure or Completion Trance:

Gestalt closure or completion *trance*s appear to be part of the hard wiring of the organism in that the nervous system constantly seeks to complete the unknown. A completion *trance* occurs when we expect someone to arrive at a particular time, and the person does not arrive. Anytime there is confusion, insufficient information, or no information, completion *trances* occur. The nervous system will begin to create answers about what has happened disregarding the fact that it has no idea what has occurred. This completion error *trance* is created in relation to past, present or future events, the meaning of other's behavior or the intentions of others. After a completion *trance* occurs, the organism is often amnesic about having created the answers. Thus, it may become part of the mapping system adding to the confabulatory nature of one's beliefs and maps. Think of all the sensory illusions there are. Most people are familiar with optical illusions, one of which is the figure-ground phenomena. In this phenomenon when you focus in one way you see a cup/chalice, and when you shift your focus, you see two people facing each other.

Example:
A. Laine's friend Kinsey has not called her about the upcoming wedding rehearsal. After some time has passed, she begins to tell herself that Kinsey no longer likes her and may have invited another friend.

B. John notices that his friend Richard is unusually quite. He starts telling himself that John must be angry with him for forgetting his birthday yesterday. After some time has passed, John begins to notice that he is feeling angry with Richard.

Examples from your experience:
(1)

(2)

---

13. *I am or Identity Trance Clusters:*

I am or identity *trance clusters* are at the core of having a particular life, particular time lines, particular expectations, dreams, hopes, or lessons to be learned. Sri Nisargadatta Maharaj once suggested to an enquirer "Wear the uniform; don't become the uniform." He also said, "You can have it as you like. You can distinguish in your life a pattern, or see merely a chain of accidents." The authors see identities as *persistent patterns of trance clusters* brought about by the structure created and imposed over reality by the *sensory perceptive holographic mapping* of the organism's nervous system. Whenever there is an "I," there is an identity, such as the "mommy" identity, the "daddy," the "teacher," the "clown," etc., There are endless examples

Examples:
A. Jane believes that in order to be a "good mother" she must do everything perfectly. She uses her grandmother Sarah as the epitome of what a mother should be.

B. George is attempting to follow a particular belief system. He believes that he must dress a certain way, eat certain foods, and only interact with certain people. In addition, he has never met anyone from this faith. He read about it in a book.

Examples from your experience:
(1)

---

(2)

Summary

Sensory perceptive alteration is essential to the creation and maintenance of *homeostasis*. Maintaining balance and congruence in a world of sensory data that is incongruent with the organism's map is an ongoing process. The adding and subtracting of sensory stimuli is critical in the creation of a s*ensory perceptive map* that stays harmonious. Therefore, confabulation and closure are two of the primary forces in h*omeostasis* that drive the need for *sensory perceptive alteration.*

Basic biological functioning is balanced and congruent until the process of *socialization* whereby the basic functions of eating, breathing, sleeping, safety, and comfort, are altered and affected by it. Stephen Wolinsky, Ph.D., a noted psychologist and author once taught, "The interruption in the outward flow of energy is what creates neurosis." The authors see what Freud termed neuroses as the development of *SPA* states not congruent with the environment and thus a disruption of the energy flow.

Ways to Change Sensory Perceptive Alteration (*SPA*)

1. Becoming aware of "hypnotic" phenomena, as discussed, and labeling it frequently leads to deconstruction of environmentally incongruent states and reconstruction of environmentally congruent states.

2. Addressing *cognitive programming errors* by utilizing "testing for programming errors" will lead to deconstruction and frequently replacement of an incongruent *SPA* with one that is environmentally congruent.

3. Utilizing diagramming, spoon-feeding, and *neural information centers* updates will change *SPA*.

4. Utilizing communication directly with *neural information centers* may change *SPA*.

5. Practicing "staying" in the present with the use of *present time sensory alignment* will deconstruct and reconstruct *SPA*.

6. Changing body postures and motor movement intertwined with the *SPA* will deconstruct *SPA*.

Explanations are meant to please the mind. They need not be true. Reality is indefinable and indescribable.
Sri Nisargadatta Maharaj

This ability of the nervous system to alter the sensory perception at its basic level makes it almost imperceptible for us to notice the shifting of information. This is further emphasized by the socialization process whereby the distortion and alterations of the group and culture are merged into the persons experience and understanding of themselves and the world.

COGNITIVE PROGRAMMING ERRORS

"You can always say more about what you have already said."
Korzybski (Science and Sanity, 1993)

Cognitive programming errors interrupt the biological process and are instrumental in the birth of neurosis and compartmentalization. (These programming errors are the way the dysfunctional teachings, instructions, directives, and cultural beliefs from family, community, ethnic group, region, country, and religion are imparted and absorbed by the organism. When programming leads to dysfunction, we call the programming, programming errors.) These *cognitive programming errors* are the cognitive distortions and archetypical errors that represent the distortions of thinking that come as the organism attempts to know, predict, and control the flow of energy through its corporeal existence. These pieces of information act as post-hypnotic suggestions and are activated during the organism's living in the environment. Keep in mind that the organism interprets these statements based on its own state of existence. Some programming errors seem to be a part of the hardwiring of the organism, such as the "completion error," the "referencing error," and positive and negative hallucinatory command errors. These types of (distortions are ways) that the organism maintains *homeostasis*, keeping the information pool the same, and maintaining the congruence of the *sensory perceptive holographic mapping system*. Confabulatory creation within the *mapping system* is the standard where there is a mixture of incoming stimuli with associational, assumptive, and referential meanings (as well as billions of stimuli filtered out and not ever integrated into the perceptive mapping system). In order for any of the *cognitive programming errors* to exist and persist, there will be the accompanying "*trance* phenomena" or *sensory perceptive alteration*s. In addition, there will be *persistent patterns of trance clusters* that the organism and others perceive as the person. The "personality illusion" appears to be a product of the programming and programming errors as they begin to interrupt the biology and fragmentation and compartmentalization of the organism occur.

Frequently Found Cognitive Programming Errors

This list is not intended to be used as an exhaustive one. Its purpose is to serve as a catalyst to promote a personal search for programming errors
1. *(CT) Comparative Thinking Errors:*

Comparing self to the following:
    A.   Existing others (brothers, sisters, parents, friends, associates)
    B.   Implied others (everybody else, them, others.)

C. Unarticulated comparison or unspoken comparative object ("It is just not good enough;" "It can be done better;" "I am an imposter.")

Examples:
(1)
_____
_____

(2)
_____
_____

2. *(PT) Polarized Thinking Errors:*

Life exists at poles or extremist thinking (success – failure, awkward – athletic, failing – A's, bad – good, totally imperfect versus perfect – poor quality vs. excellent)

Examples:
(1)
_____
_____

(2)
_____
_____

3. *(DC) Discounting Errors:*

Subtracting from or reducing the actual positive contribution or input, you have made in defiance of objective reality ("You got an A on the test." "Yes, but the professor was very easy.")

Examples:
(1)
_____
_____

(2)
_____
_____

4. *(RT) Regressed Thinking Errors*:

RT is seeing current events interwoven with past events. ("Every time I come into this office now, I feel sad. I remember the day Jim was fired.")

Examples:
(1)
_____
_____

(2)
_____
_____

5. *(FP) Future Projection Errors:*

FP is to negate segments of the present with statements or visualizations about a possible future. ("I can't enjoy my vacation for picturing the board meeting next week.")

Examples:
(1)
_____
_____

(2)
_____
_____

6. *(NHCE) Negative Hallucinatory Command Errors*:

NHCE are self-programming leading to perceptual deletions in defiance of reality. ("There is nothing good about Frank." – Speaker deletes witnessed acts of kindness to friends and his children.)

Examples:

(1)

(2)

7. *(PHCE) Positive Hallucinatory Command Errors*:

PHCE is self-programming leading to perceptual additions that are of a visual, auditory, and even tactile or propriorceptive nature in defiance of reality. ("Lillian stared at me." vs. "Lillian looked in my direction." "They were laughing at me." vs. "Joe and Jim were in the corner of the room laughing about something.")

Examples:

(1)

(2)

8. *(ECE): External Control Errors*:

ECE is self programming which states that our feelings are externally created, controlled, and sustained rather than a product of ourselves ("They make me so angry.")

Examples:
(1)

_____

_____

(2)

_____

_____

9.   (ATE): *Assumptive Thinking Errors:*

ATE is assuming that you know what someone else is thinking or meaning without clear communications from them concerning what their intent or meaning is to you.

Examples:
(1)

_____

_____

(2)

_____

_____

10. (*MTE*): *Magical Thinking Errors:*

Magical thinking errors is telling oneself that something is going to produce a certain outcome without a clear, logical chain of events moving toward that end. ("Even though I am not studying, somehow I will pass the test," or "No matter what I do, I cannot succeed. I'm cursed.")

Examples:
(1)

_____

_____

(2)

_____

11. *(OOE) Only One Errors:*

Self-programming which indicates you are alone in your experience – ("No one else has ever done this, felt this, and had this experience.")

Examples:
(1)

(2)

12. *(NLE) Negative Label Errors:*

Although labels are a useful part of language, to label something is also to limit. For instance, once an object is labeled as a fruit it automatically excludes any uses of it as a hand tool, vehicle, book, etc. Applications of negative labels serve the same limiting function. To label oneself as a "loser" automatically limits his perception of the time that he has succeeded or won. Once the limit is established, it limits opportunities that are not consistent with the label. (i.e. "I do not apply for promotions. I do not enter contests.") Please note this programming error frequently operates in tandem with negative hallucinatory command errors and/or discounting errors.

Examples:
(1)

(2)

13. *(NCE) No Choice Errors:*

Self-programming which endorses that the individual had no choice or no alternatives, and therefore is not responsible for the consequences of his actions or is a victim.
Examples:
(1)

(2)

14. *(TPE) Trapped by the Past Errors*:

Self-programming whose message is "I cannot move to a different future course because I am stuck with or within the past. I am trapped by history in a set mold."
Examples:
(1)

(2)

15. *(GE) Best Not Good Enough Errors*:

Despite objective evidence that the individual exerted maximal effort, he tells himself that he should have done better. **Examples:**
(1)

(2)

16. (SOE) Should/Ought Errors:

Should have (should have not statements) which imply the existence of all necessary factors to cause an action. (An apple, given appropriate levels of moisture and temperature, should fall from a tree, and it does. Mary is angry with Jim because she tells herself that Jim should see things the way she does, but he obviously does not.)

Examples:
(1)

(2)

17. (RE) Reference Errors:

Self-programming that leads the individual to think that everything is about him/her. That the actions of others are in reference to him. Carl states, "Just like the Christmas party, they cancelled the dance to keep me from socializing with them."

Examples:
(1)

(2)

18. (CE/GE) Completion Errors/Gestalt Closure Errors:

When there is insufficient information or no information to render a judgment, the individual fills in the blanks. Your friend has not shown up for lunch, you have no information as to why, so you begin to tell yourself what might have happened and believe it to be true. This type of error may involve associational, assumptive, or referential searches to fill in the information. Frequently (CE/GE) errors will present in the form of two subtypes a) Extrapolative (Ext) and b) Interpolation (Int).(Ext) errors involve projections into the future based on inadequate sampling for such projections.(Int) errors involve filling in the blank as in the above example. A classic form of an (Ext) error would be, "I was turned down by the first college I applied to, therefore any college in the future I apply to will turn me down."

Examples:
(1)

(2)

19. *(EE) Expectation Errors/Contractual Thinking Errors*

Self-programming where the individual tells himself that certain things will occur because of something he has done. ("If I am nice to others, they will be nice to me.") This is often the source of confusion and resentment.

Examples:
(1)

(2)

20. *(KE) Knowledge Errors*:

This is the type of error that influences an individual to believe that there is special knowledge about existence, the world, and about things in it the world and if a person has, the correct knowledge then he will always make the perfect decision. (Helen reports, "If only my father had lived to advise me, I would not be in this bad marriage.")

Examples:
(1)
_____
_____

(2)
_____
_____

21. *(OA) Overly Attributive:*

Programming that exaggerates the accomplishments, power, and even magnitude of others or task at hand. (Client, "My father was a great man. He completed college and worked forty hours a week to accomplish this feat." (Therapist) "So did you, Bob. Can you see your accomplishments?"

"Or I feel so depressed. When I look at the sink, the dishes are like mountains."

"Or whenever I must confront the people at the car dealership, they look like giants to me."

Examples:
(1)
_____
_____

(2)
_____
_____

22. (DE) Descartes' Error:

This error occurs when one separates the mind/body and speaks as if it were two different things. Along with this error is the error of dividing a person into thoughts versus feelings. The compartmentalization of the various aspects of experience into separate areas of the body subdivides the person and his experience. This dividing of the organism leads to the debate, over which is primary, most important, or has origination, and is therefore causative.

Examples:
(1)

(2)

The interaction of *sensory alteration* with the *post hypnotic effect* of *socialization* creates a confabulatory mapping experience, where the projective overlay of the system with its effects on the person's experience of the reality is quite extensive and almost undetectable.
The loop effect of perception from the observer to the observed appears and is experienced as if it were interpersonal, but in fact it is primarily intrapersonal. People places, things, and experiences appear in the conceptual world but they are not there. Everything is actually taking place in the hologram of the internally created mapping system; it is only through focused awareness that one can pierce the illusion and notice that everyone in his or her own hologram.

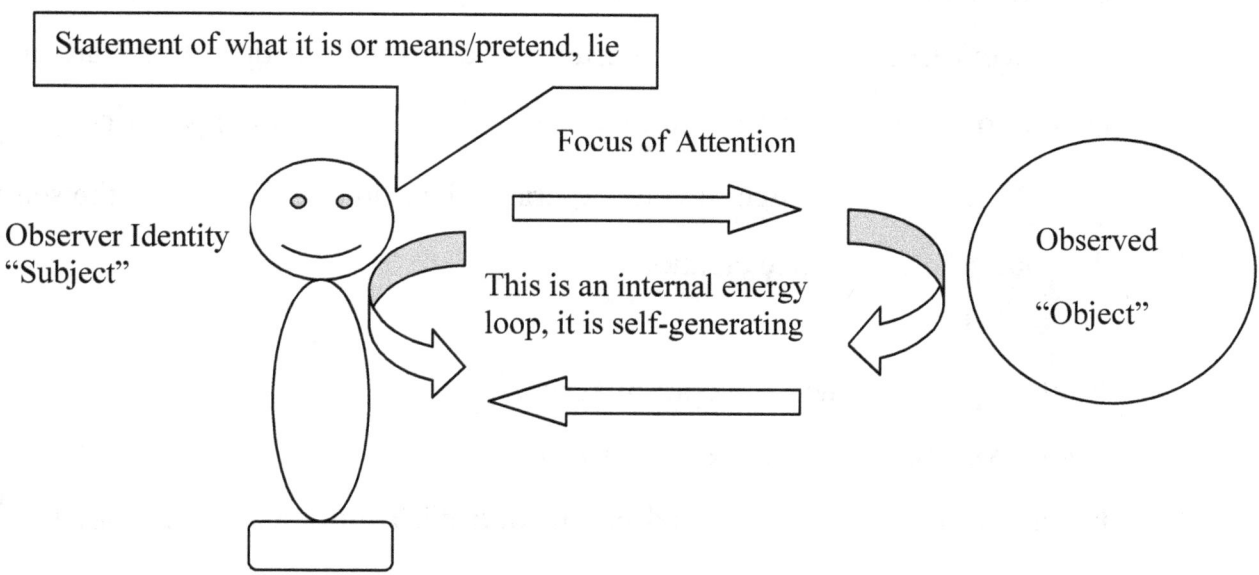

Some questions that can be useful are:

What am I focusing on or paying attention to? (Image, thought, feeling, person, place, thing or some aspect of energy, mass, or space-time).
What am I saying it is or means?
By saying that it means that (X), what am I wanting, creating, expecting?
By "wanting, creating, expecting, believing…" That, what am I resisting?
Or what did you assume, decide or believe that got you to creating that?

Notice or allow yourself to be aware of any shifts in your physiology or mental space. Become aware of any changes in breathing, muscle tension {energy blocks and flow} numbness or other feelings.

Each time there is observation it is another position, window, portal, framework through which to experience the infinite through. There are an infinite or enumerable amount of variations in observational positions.

The "**I am**" is the source of your experiential world and the love of the self is the source of experience creation.

Each experience will have an observer.
Each experience will have a location.
Each experience will be fused or imbued with some aspect of energy, mass or space-time.

The I is a dimensionless point of awareness. You are not awareness you are what awareness appears on. The real is beyond description or experience.

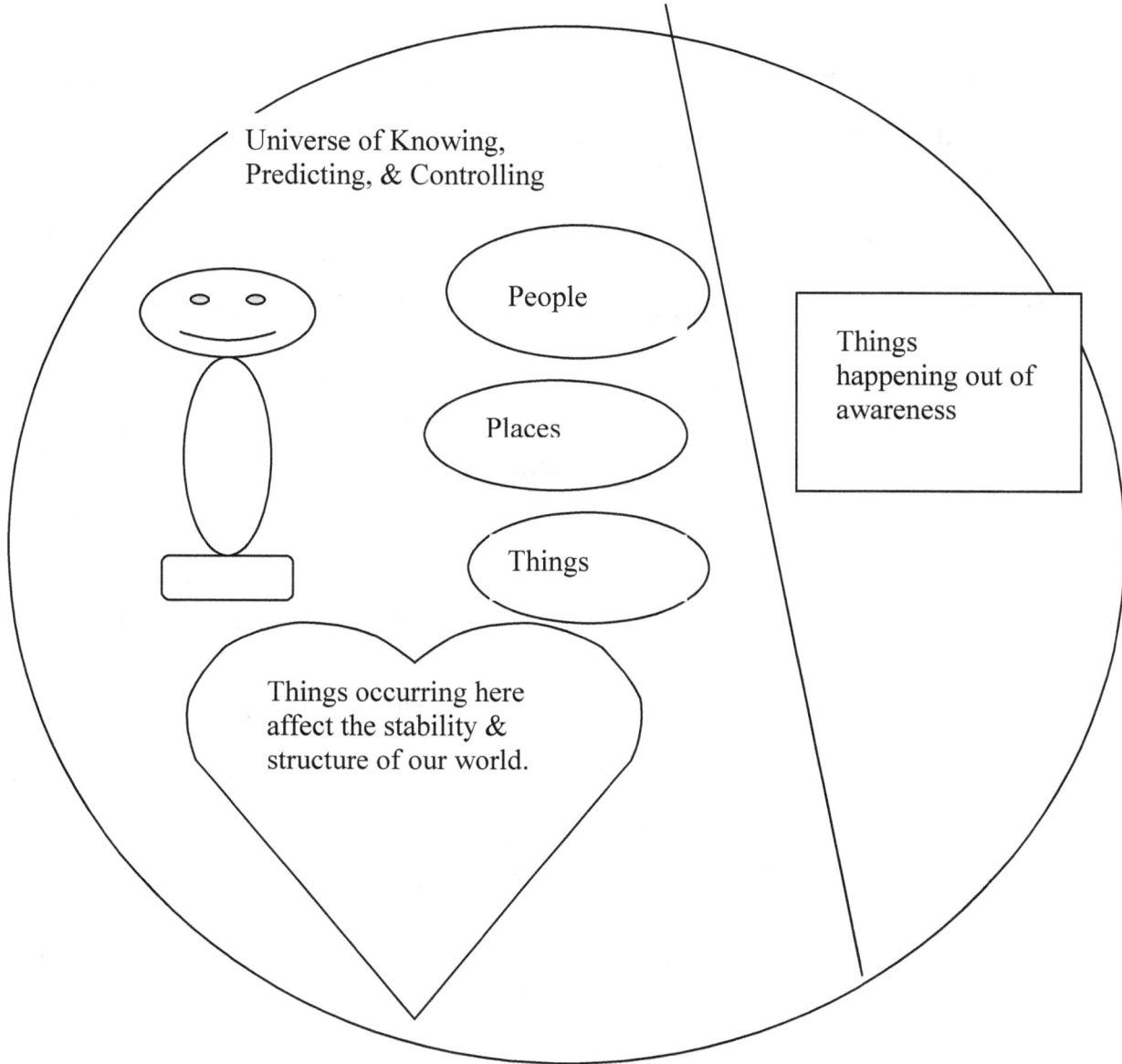

The first labeled experience will generally be the point of reference. This creates a frozen window of meaning, where the focus of attention will be fixated until it is released. Alteration of any aspect of the window will create universal shifts in meaning and experience. Observers are windows of strategy, meaning, and experiences, while the identities are further fused with the experience. Each experience is contained in your universe. You cannot explain personal experiences to others .

Also keep in mind we often have fusion of meanings that will confuse what things are. Like love = respect.

Question for yourself what it means or doesn't mean, when words are merged and then separated.

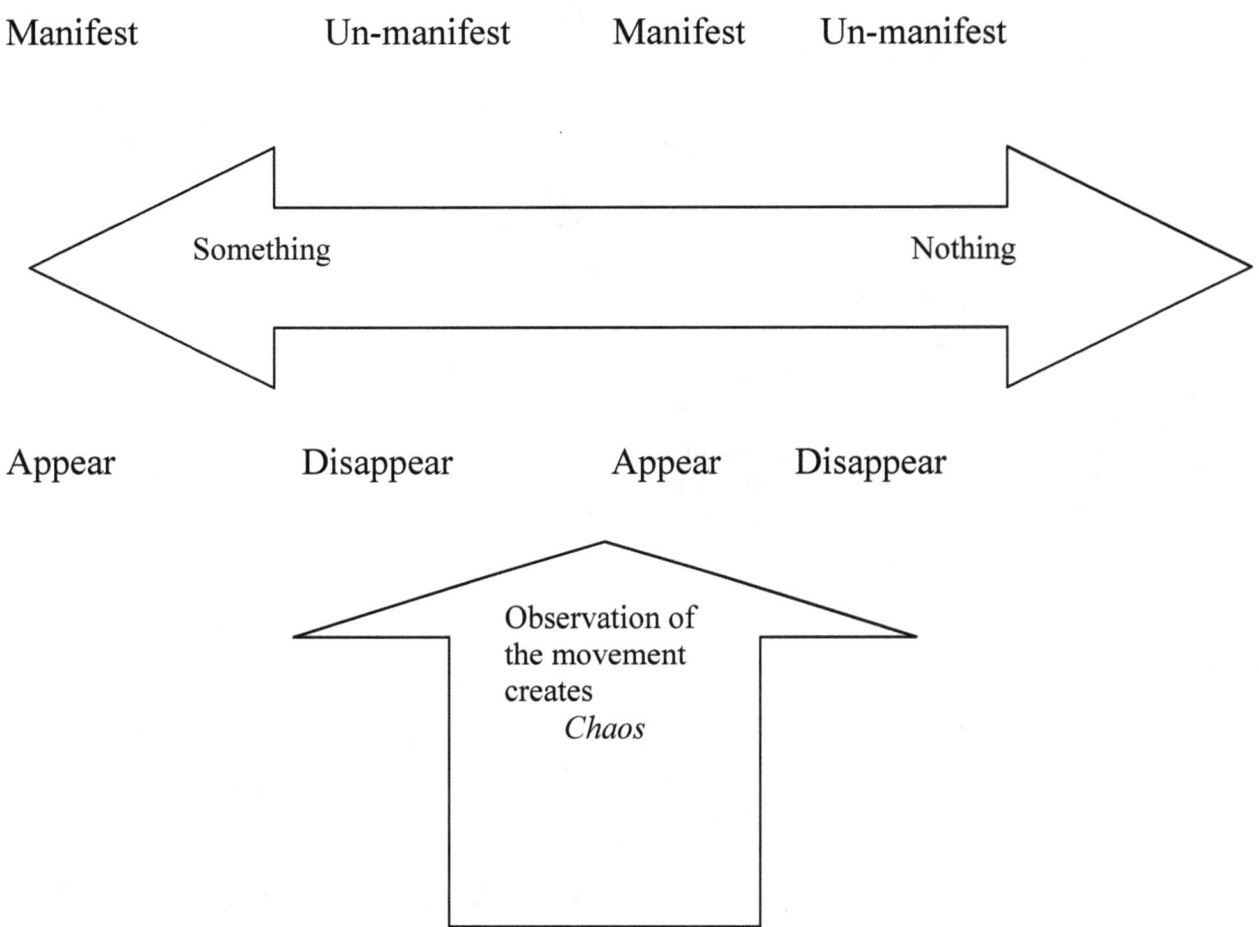

Essence or the clear space is able to merge with its creations. By dividing its attention duality is experienced and there is an observer and an observed. Within the Sensory Perceptive Holographic Interactive Mapping System, a world is created and experienced as being real. By forgetting that it is created and then pretending we did not create it and further pretending that we are not pretending, we forget. The I am forgets that its nature is beyond the creator/creating/created identities and that it is the source of the conceptual world and its meaning. In Quantum Psychology, we learn:

1. Observation creates the experience of reality.

2. Everything interpenetrates everything. There is only one substance.

3. Everything is emptiness, form is condensed emptiness. There is nothing.

4. There is non-local causality/faster than light communication/connection. There are no causes.

Maintain flexible focus of attention and awareness that everything appears within consciousness, nothing exists outside of consciousness, and consciousness is not it.

People have a limited number of physical and psychological postures."
George Gurdjieff, The Gurdjieff Factor

As we begin to explore deeper into the nature of *homeostasis* and *sensory perceptive holographic mapping*, there is often a question about personality and the core nature of the organism. Personality is an illusion in that we assume because we see some patterns of response that the individual is always that way. Trance clusters are those groupings of responses that manifest as part of the ongoing repetition in the sensory perceptive world and are triggered in stimulus response scenarios. The temporary and transient nature of personality is observed if there is some illness or injury to the organism. People often make statements such as "I'm just not myself today." On the other hand, they make inaccurate statements, like "I always tell the truth," or "I never forget to clean the house." These are all ways that we deny the inconsistencies or variations in the ways we act and attempt to maintain the illusion of sameness, congruence, and *homeostasis*. Some very interesting reading can be found in the works of Antonia Damasio in both *"Descartes' Error"* and in *"Looking for "Spinoza"*. These works explore the neuro-physiological, biochemical underpinnings of mind/body, thought, feeling, and emotion construction from a biological and philosophical view. The illusion of a unified person is part of the biological response to the mind/body's interaction with the living environment of which it is a part. We are now beginning to be able to study and explain the complex interaction of thoughts, feelings and emotions as part of the total organism and its continuum of responses to internal and external stimuli. These interrelated manifestations of biological responses as demonstrated in our patterns of behavior are more readily explained by the on going patterns of neural mapping and networking, than a fixed construct of a personality structure.

Identity Creation

There are an infinite number of identities created, as they spontaneously appear with each experience and disappear when the experience is over. Identities are a construction within the *sensory perceptive holographic mapping system* as part of the nervous system's effort to organize chaos. The nervous system uses identities to deal with the feeling of being out of control, not knowing, being overwhelmed, or the fear of disappearance (annihilation). As you go through life, you may notice that people, places, things, experiences, thoughts, feelings, and really everything appears and disappears. Some things last longer than others do. Some things appear for millennia, while other things are here for a nanosecond. The mind/body gains skills to meet its needs. It learns these skills from others (parents, siblings, teachers, and others) by observation, instruction, or accident. In taking on the behaviors or mannerisms of others, the person may do this by modeling what is observed or by being instructed. He can fuse with what is observed, or he may resist that behavior or tact and develop what appears to be the opposite. Remember, that in observing others the underlying motives, intentions, or needs are not known, so external behaviors may be duplicated without understanding the internal mechanisms.

The fear of disappearance creates the *need to know* which prompts the mind/body to create the *mapping system* with an illusionary world that is *knowable, predictable, and controllable.* The mind/body has to abstract the sensory information in the environment because of its inability to accurately sense and assimilate all of the stimuli available. There are limitations to the abilities of the sense organs, themselves. Thus, distortions occur due to the inability to accurately detect or sense environmental stimuli. The limited sensory information is then deleted, distorted, generalized, added to, and confabulated in order to make it knowable, predictable, and controllable. Confabulation here is to indicate that sensory information from the environment is mixed with information from within the *mapping system*. The Gestalt closure phenomenon is an example of when the organism answers its own questions in order to fill in a blank area in information. The nervous system decides what to know and what not to know thus editing the sensory information to make it congruent with the *mapping system* already in place. Adding and subtracting the various elements that make up the mosaic of life makes interpretation quite fluid and malleable.

"I"dentities Are:

Identities are biologically encoded response strategies to stimuli encountered in the environment as mediated by the *sensory perceptive holographic mapping system* and shaped by the *socialization* process. Identities are conceptual frameworks that are imposed over the biological core of the organism during the *socialization* process. Prior to the *socialization* experiences, the organism had no conceptual frameworks interfering or altering its experience with the environment. The acquisition of identities occurs during the interactions with mom, dad and others as the developing person seeks to meet biological and interpersonal needs that are required for survival. These identities can be described as roles, positions, points of view, *trances* (*SPA*s), strategies, frames of reference, and *persistent patterns of trance clusters*. Each of these descriptions can be further explained as to their functions.

Roles are prescribed patterns of social behavior and interactive rules of behavior, such as son, daughter, mother, father, cousin, husband, wife, businessman, deacon in a church, counselor or, teacher. These roles may be learned in the family, in the community, or prescribed by the society, religious or social group.

Positions refer to a defined point in reference to others. These positions can be points of reference such as young rather than old, happy as opposed to sad, good as juxtaposition to bad, democrat rather than libertarian or republican.

Identities as strategies can be described as the ways we think, feel and behave in order to meet some need or want. Identities always reference the philosophical core (the central belief about life); that is supported by the various belief systems of the individual and carried out in the form of strategies. Needs and wants may include but are not limited to food, shelter, safety, learning, love, sanity, knowing, or being in control. Being the "good son," the "cute daughter," the "faithful servant" are all different types of strategies. Strategies can be learned by interacting and observing others interacting. They can be developed by trying to be like others or by being the opposite of others or even some combination of the behaviors used by others.

Persistent patterns of trance clusters are those identities, roles positions (psychological, physiological, and philosophical) and strategies that are most often demonstrated by the individual, observed, and recognized by others as their persona or personality.

Dr. Stephen Wolinsky an expert in identity and trance states said, "You will suffer to the degree that you believe that you are your identities." He also said, "You don't have problems, your identities do." (Personal telephone conversation, June 2005). If identities are viewed as frames of reference or strategies then they can be seen as flexible and changeable. Identities only become problematic when they become frozen, fixed or when we are fused with them and refuse to or cannot detach from them. Sri Nisargadatta Maharaj said, "Pain is merely a signal that the body is in danger and requires attention. Similarly, suffering warns us that the structure of memories and habits, which we call the person, is threatened by loss or change. Pain is essential for the survival of the body, but none compels you to suffer. Suffering is due entirely to clinging or resisting; it is a sign of our unwillingness to move on, to flow with life" (I Am That, Sri Nisargadatta Maharaj, 1973).

There is a Sanskrit saying that is useful to keep in mind as it relates to the *Identity* and the *sensory perceptive holographic mapping system* or the world of the person. The saying is *Dristi, Shristi, Vada*, "The world is only there as long as there is an "I" there to perceive it." (The Supreme Yoga, Swami Venkatesananda, 1976). As we begin to explore the identities that appear and disappear within the m*apping system* keep in mind that the map is not the territory and the identity is not the person

Posture, Breathing and Eye Movement are Part of the Pattern

The physical postures of the body match or pace with the identity's internal pictures. Pauses and shifts in breathing indicate alterations in emotions, feelings or other internal states. As the Neuro Linguistic programmers learned from Milton Erickson, M.D., eye movements may give a lot of information about internal states. There is at least anecdotal data to indicate that eye movement may give clues to the sense being used to access or create information. The patterns are idiosyncratic but can be useful when there is out of awareness sensory accessing. An example of out of awareness sensory accessing is when an individual may be utilizing visual images or auditory sounds without being consciously aware.

Jennette says that she is remembering how her mother disciplined her because she can see an image of a time that happened. As you notice her eye movement, it appears that she is also responding to some inner dialogue or sounds and when you ask her what she is saying to herself or listening to, she says she can also hear her mother's voice. Additionally, she notices a kinesthetic response of a knot in her stomach.

The eye-accessing chart on the next page comes from a compilation of examples found in the works of. Steve Lankton, MSW. <u>Practical Magic</u>, 1980; Bobby Bodenhammer, <u>The User's Manual For the Brain</u>, 1999; and The <u>Neuro-Linguistic Programming Home Study Guide</u>, developed by David Gordon, Leslie Cameron-Bandler and Michael Lebeau, 1984.

The chart gives some suggestions as to what sensory area or apparatus is being accessed when the eyes move in certain directions or into certain positions. These eye movements give clues and hints to the mapping area that is being used when creating or remembering information

Eye Accessing Cues

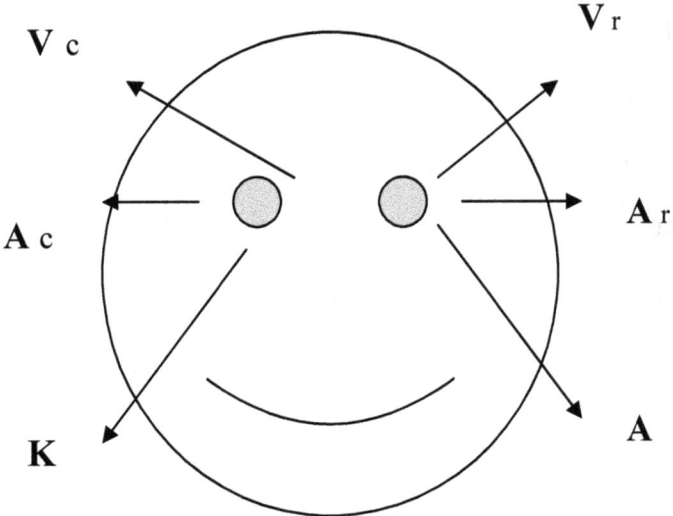

V c = Visual constructed images
V r = (remembered eidetic) image
(Eyes defocused and unmoving also indicates visual accessing.)
A c = Auditory constructed words or sounds
A r = Auditory remembered sounds or words
K = Kinesthetic feelings (also smell and taste)
A = Auditory sounds or words

These are Visual accessing cues for a "normally organized" right-handed person

People will say that they are "visual," "auditory" or "hands on learners" when in fact all senses are being used when experiencing life. Individuals may have modes of perception that they prefer, are most familiar and find it easiest to use when describing their experiences. More information can be found concerning eye movement in the works of Richard Bandler and John Grinder, the founders of Neuro Linguistic Programming.

Intrapersonal Nature of Identity

Identities appear to be interpersonal or interactive but most of what is going on is intrapersonal in nature. Although there appears to be an observer identity, in actuality there is only *observing* taking place. The *observing* creates the *observer* and the *observed*. Below there are several different types of identity labels to explore and experience.

Identities

Hearer	*Hearing*	*Heard*
Seer	*Seeing*	*Seen*
Observer	*Observing*	*Observed*
Feeler	*Feeling*	*Felt*
Thinker	*Thinking*	*Thought*

Identity's Intrapersonal Loop

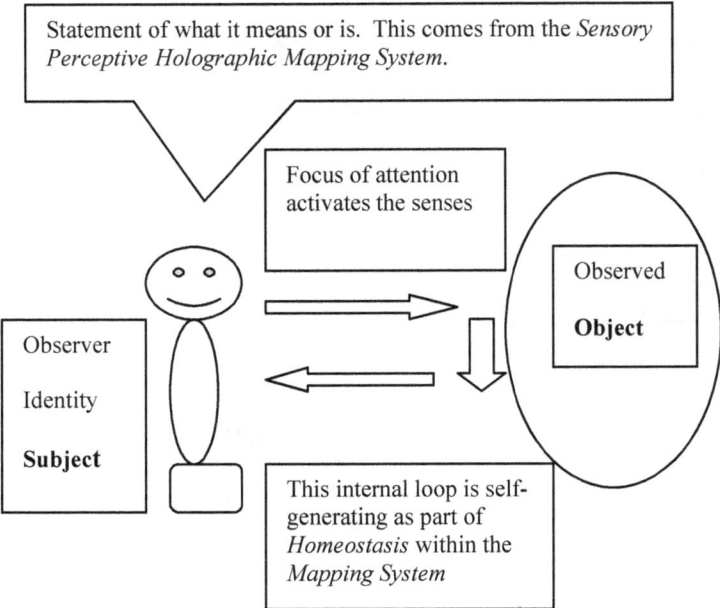

The observer identity appears simultaneously with the object it observes and then goes inside to access the meaning of the object from within the *mapping system*. Therefore, what starts as an interpersonal interaction ends up as an intrapersonal interaction.

Questions for Identities (Trance States)

In each identity or observer identity, you wish to explore or examine, ask the following questions.

What am I paying attention to or what am I focusing on? (Image, thought, feeling, person, place, thing, energy, space, mass or time.)

What am I saying that it is or means?

By saying that it, means (X) that what am I wanting, creating, doing, or expecting. (Also, not doing, not wanting, not creating, not expecting?)

By wanting all of the above, what am I resisting?

Notice shifts or changes in your physiology, primarily breathing.

Watch for energy flow or blocks in the body (muscle tension, numbness etc.)

Let the experience dissolve in whatever way is comfortable for you.

Notice that each "observer identity" is a different window into a universe that has its own unique meaning and experiences.

You are the source of your experiential world.

Identities are a unique response to the stimuli as interpreted in the context of the nervous system's *sensory perceptive holographic mapping system*. The first created association or meaning will be the meaning and association that remains primary and will be accessed when similar stimuli are encountered. Alteration of any aspect of sensory perception will cause shifts in the meaning, association, and what is experienced. This is one reason for the activation of *SPA* states that maintain the appearance of congruence within the mapping world.

SEMANTIC REVERSALS

"The opposite of what we say and hear is often what is true."
Unknown

Problems can occur when there are mixed or confused messages contained in the *neural information centers* that are a part of the *sensory perceptive holographic mapping system*. Mirroring responses are those responses that result when the projections or introjections are confused, and the location of the reference becomes mixed up. An example of this confusion can be when an individual cannot see himself as being successful or competent due to programming errors. *Semantic reversal mechanisms* are a part of the *homeostatic* system that is designed to protect the *sensory perceptive mapping system*. Their function is to neutralize incoming information that threatens *dissonance* to the organism. These mechanisms may involve semantic reversals of the incoming stimuli, such as the addition of "not" and the inclusion of "yes, but" formulations and pseudo-logical argumentations. Further, they can be visual with images that attempt to counter the incoming threatening information.

Mind/Body Inclusion

This discussion emphasizes that the mind/body is one, and as this theoretical model unfolds, it is clear that the entire organism is included. Mind/body integration and inclusion move our thinking and awareness beyond the divisive errors of Descartes' reasoning when he divided the organism into separate parts and created an artificial barrier in the unity of the organism. This arbitrary division of the organism is an illusion created by language, and it further leads to the separation of thoughts, feelings, and emotions. *Neural information centers* contain and may abstract symbolic representations of sensory stimuli, such as color, sound, texture, odor, and smell, as well as the various distinctions within and between these sensory typologies. The words that represent these are visual, auditory, tactile, olfactory and gustatory. The mind/body encodes this data and references and/or associates present stimuli with earlier or variant stimuli as encoded within the experienced neuro-chemical mapping system. Kinesthetics are a subset of proprioception, which is the recognition of organs and body organization, placement, and sensation within the spatial world of the organism. Vestibular orientation places the mind/body in harmony and balance with gravity. Kinesthetics appear to be the internal orientation and recognition response as noted by alterations within the physiology to position the organism as to approach/avoidance or neutrality in relation to the stimulus field. The fight, flight or freeze response is contained within this response set. Curiosity may also be within this orientation approach.

Energy, mass, and space-time are experienced, represented, and created by the flow of "energy" or "sensory data" through the organism. Sensory stimuli as they are experienced, associated, and/or referenced within the sensory perceptive mapping system are rapidly converted to an organic response of energetic orientation that is labeled as a feeling or emotion. This represents the energetic potentiality of the mind/body in relation to its stimulus mapping. Contained within the *mapping system* are references and associations to original, past objects and the emotional connection or response to them. Visual and/or auditory stimuli are rapidly converted to kinesthetic response. The changes in heartbeat, respiration, digestion, hypothalamic changes, muscles tensing and relaxing as well as a myriad of other changes, are all part of a harmonious, concerted effort to maintain *homeostasis* and survival.

Referencing within the organism creates a looping mechanism of orientation to incoming stimuli, as well as its own response to the incoming stimuli. Stimuli are associated and referenced with the *sensory perceptive mapping system* as the pool of *neural information centers* and center programming sensitizes the organism to varying levels of neuro/biochemical change within the organism at different states of energetic potentiality. Gestalt closure is an integral part of this referencing and associating within the *mapping system*. The biological system responds to stimuli by referencing previously experienced "models" and then projecting outcomes, associations, possibilities, and the emotional states aligned with these experiences, both future and past, to notate the present experience. This again indicates the internal looping of the individual's world and world experience.

IDENTITY & THE DIAMOND OF AWARENESS

"This is the mystery of imagination that it seems to be so real. You may be celibate or married, a monk or a family man; that is not the point. Are you a slave to your imagination or are you not? Whatever decision you take, whatever work you do will invariably be based on imagination, on assumptions parading as facts."
(<u>I Am That</u>, Sri Nisargadatta Maharaj, 1973)

The Diamond of Awareness is the name for a method of *present time sensory alignment* that includes considerations of how we describe and experience energy, time, space, and mass. All location is relative to position. From the point of where we are, all distance is measured and perceived. We are the central focal point from which all things are perceived. This way of observing how we experience and label life is a way to create interruptions in the conscious framework and to increase the possibility of our awareness of the ongoing "*trances*" or "*SPAs*" that shape our perceptions and interactions with the self and others. The sense or concept of "I AM" precedes and necessitates all other concepts. It is the seed of the universal experience. This is the source of our world experience. By creating awareness of our abstractions, we can begin the journey back before the creation of the identity through the various concepts, feelings, and sensations to a place that is freer from programming, *cognitive programming errors*, and dysfunctional *trances*.

To begin, we start at the "I" which is our sense of presence, and then *I AM*, which is noticing one's sense of consciousness and the recognition of existence. *I Am Here* references the notation of location being here rather than anywhere else. It is the source position from which to notice other things. To be here, we cannot be there. *I Am Here Now* notates now rather than in the past or future.

The diamond is a beautiful stone when cut and polished especially when the debris is cleared away. The diamond is one of the hardest substances known to man and can be used to cut other hard substances. The Diamond of Awareness can be used to clear away all that is not part of the essential self and clear away the illusion created by the nervous system. There are three major sections of this Diamond. They are I *Am*, I Am H*ere,* and I Am *Now*. Coinciding with these are three areas of illusion or trance created by the nervous system's programming and programming errors as influenced by the *socialization* process. These three areas are I Am *this* or *that*, I Am *There,* and I Am *past* or *future*. Sri Nisargadatta Maharaj, a rogue Hindu Saint stated, "Most of what you know about yourself came from outside of you. Discard it." Before deciding which descriptors to discard, it may be useful to first notice what they are and where they came from. Maharaj also instructed, "To find out what you are, you must first find out what you are not." (I Am That, Sri Nisargadatta Maharaj 1973). When we speak of discarding, we are simply referring to examining, exploring, or stepping back from the particular identity structure. As we begin to explore the identities in their various shapes and sizes there are several things to consider as we try different exercises. Not every exercise is for everyone, so try different things, keep whatever is useful at the time, and leave what is not useful behind. If something seems confusing try it again, if it is still confusing, keep going. You can come back to it later if needed.

Confusion means to fuse with some aspect of the experience or belief. The identity (*SPA*), position, or frame of reference you are knowingly or unknowingly in could be fused with and distorting the perception or experience of another area of the territory. It may be necessary to stay with the experience to burn off excess energy or attachments. The willingness to stay with the confusion initially could be beneficial. Trying to get "clear," "enlightened," or to know is also a position and an identity.

As we start to investigate the identities, *trances* (*SPA*s), reference points, frames, or lenses, the exercises are not designed to create a better, clearer, more beneficial "I". The exercises may expand awareness or loosen associations, assumptions, and references.

When we talk about frames of reference, positions, associations, assumptions, *trances* and ask that we create a frame, this means to move through and away from the concepts and abstractions about the experience toward the original stimuli. Then step back from the stimuli and observe anew. When we reframe this means to experience the stimuli from a different perspective, filter, position, or angle. To de-frame is to step away from all known frames of reference.

I Am: This or That

The I Am this or that applies to the descriptors of the "I," and along with the description comes the categorization and judgment of the descriptor. To become clearer about the *descriptors,* one must notice if they have *judgment, preference, or significance* attached to them. Notice if any description appears automatically, and if so, where did it come from? Notice who or what authority the descriptor may have come from. Often we describe ourselves on a continuum or in polarities. The list below is just a small sampling of descriptors to start you thinking.

Descriptors

Tall
Short
Thin
Blonde
Red haired
Brunette
Hairy
Bald
Green eyes
Hazel eyes
Strong
Smart
Man
Woman
Child
Adult

These descriptors may be placed in pairs that are seen as polarities. When these polarities are interpreted to be in binaries, they are viewed as one being superior or preferred to the other. At times, they are seen as dichotomous.

Descriptors

Short -----------------------Tall
Fat------------------------Thin
Brunette---------------------Blonde
Weak----------------------Strong
Dumb----------------------Smart
American---------------------Latino
Black------------------------White

As you begin to go through these descriptors, notice which may apply to the way you describe yourself or others. Then ask yourself, or notice if there are judgments, preferences, or significances associated or fused with the descriptors. There are often evaluators paired with descriptors. *Evaluators* give the descriptor a value judgment, which may be in either a positive or a negative direction. Some evaluators are words like.

Evaluators

Good --------------------------Bad
Right --------------------------Wrong
Should------------------------Should not

If you notice that there are judgments, preferences, or significances associated with the descriptors, ask yourself who or what authority told you that. If you notice whom it came from, then notice how you decided that it was true. Ask yourself what you assumed, decided, or believed to get you to create that association.

What does it mean to have judgment, preference, or significance associated with a descriptor? Judgment is indicated by labeling something as good or bad, right or wrong, positive or negative, superior or inferior. When we say that some quality, trait, or description is something that is either an enhancement or a deficit, we are issuing a judgment. *Bill is very strong, but that is not a good quality for an artist.* Preference is noted when one trait, quality, or attribute is seen as superior or inferior to another. Being thin is a desirable trait but to be slender is much preferred. *Susan's musical ability is far more useful than Mary's dancing.* Significance is applied when it is seen as more or less important to have or not have certain identified traits, qualities, or abilities. *Isn't it wonderful that Kristie has such a brilliant sense of design?*

Dr. Stephen Wolinsky, noted identity and *trance* expert, presented the following formulation: That "I" + (word-descriptor) = identity (Personal telephone Conversation, August 2005). One example could be *I am a man*, or *I am happy*. A fusion of meanings can occur when we say "**X**" means "**Y**". We associate meanings and then forget that we associated them, we then believe the associations to be true. An example of this could be, *I am a man, and therefore, I must be strong and confident.* We begin by pretending X, and then pretend that we are not pretending. Therefore, we become that in our *mapping system.* Remember, most of what you know about yourself came from outside of you, therefore discard it. This means that we may want to examine this knowledge or explore its origins and meanings further. Others tell us who we are, should be, or need to be. We are then told how to act, and what our actions or statements mean.

Words as Containers of Experiential and Associational Meaning

As we explore the world of words, we need to keep in mind that words are abstractions. As we move away from the original sensations into images, emotions, feelings, and word descriptions, we are moving further and further from the original stimulus-sensation and therefore the meaning is more abstracted. Words create their own world of meanings and associations. Words are unique to the experiences and connections of the individual and the environment that he has been exposed to. When a young child is told *the stove is hot,* he reaches out to touch the stove because without the experience of what hot is, the word "hot" has no reference, or associational meaning. The next exposure to the word "hot" will bring new adjusted responses. For just a moment, think of all the words that have multiple meanings, depending on the spelling or the context of how they are used. Words like *bear or bare, see or sea, and here or hear.* Words like love, hot, bad, mother, and father (etc.) have varying meanings and associations. Each individual accesses different experiential, associational, and emotional references for any word. That is part of the miracle and complexity of language.

Communication is difficult and errors in interpretation and understanding occur frequently.

Words are part of a complex symbolic representation system that attempts to describe and explain what happens in the individual's *sensory perceptive mapping system.* Some writers such as Wittgenstein and Derrida have described words as, simply referring to other words and as part of a complex game that defers its explanations to other abstract representations and never reaches the concrete level of the territory. (<u>On Certainty</u>, Wittgenstein, 1969).

Remember the representations in your mapping world are symbols and are not the territory. Words can be used as descriptors, they can serve as evaluators, and some words can act as *modifiers* that shift or alter the meaning of the word. Modifiers can be words like *very, extremely, not, barely, and hardly.* Words have different meanings depending on the individual, family, social group, culture, or time. Words are used as if they never vary in meaning, and as if the object or experience the word describes is the same thing as the word and interchangeable with the word. The word and the thing it refers to are not the same thing. For example, the *word "apple" cannot be eaten. You cannot sit in the word "chair." You will not swim in the word "sea," nor can you breathe the word "air."*

Next, we will begin to explore descriptors, evaluators and where they came from within the *sensory perceptive mapping system.*

I Am This or That: Exercise

List your *descriptors*, then list any *evaluators* then list *who or what authority* said them.

Descriptor	Evaluator	Who or What Authority	
_____	_____	_____	_____
_____	_____	_____	_____
_____	_____	_____	_____

As you become aware of an identity you assume, then become aware who or what authority made that statement or gave you that example. Become aware that we believed that we knew the meaning, motivation, and intent of the person, when in fact we may not have known.

Identity Exercise

Find an identity that you wish to explore. The identity may have a positive or negative association for you. We suggest that you do not pick your most difficult identity or the most traumatic. An example could be I am a mother-identity; I am a counselor-identity; I am happy-identity.

When you select an identity, create the identity. Merge with the identity by stepping into it. Experience it in whatever way you do that. Then detach by stepping out of it.

(This helps us to notice if we are associated or dissociated with the identity) If you cannot step into it then you are experiencing some dissociation.

If you step in but have difficulty stepping out of it, you are experiencing being overly associated. You may need to experience it more to burn off the excess energy of attachment.

Notice who or what authority told you that or modeled that for you.

Listen for the voice and various elements of sound, tone, loudness.

Look for any images, and other visual attributes such as colors, black and white, and distance.

Be aware of any sensations and the various elements of kinesthetic or tactile sense representation intensity and duration. Notice if there is any numbness or lack of sensation.

Where do you experience this identity, notice the location in the physical body, face or head.

Notice any energy. Does the energy seem to have movement or does the energy seem to be frozen. If there is movement, is it fast or slow and in what direction. Now step into the identity frame, now change the frame.

Now de-frame, and notice what changes.

Enneagram Fixations

The Sufis, who are Middle Eastern wise men, developed an ancient system for identifying nine personality fixations called the Enneagram. These nine fixations are false identifications that result in attempts to compensate for the fixation. Keep in mind that anything you think you are, you are not. False conclusions lead to false solutions. The Enneagram is similar to the Meyers-Briggs Personality Inventory, which looks at personality types, preferences, or styles. This work looks at *persistent patterns of trance clusters* as a way of meeting needs and the structuralization of the energetic space that appears as a personality.

Enneagram Fixations
Perfection
Will
Harmony
Origin
Omniscience
Strength
Truth
Wisdom
Love

Enneagram Fixations and their Compensators

Perfect----------------------------------Imperfect
Worthy-----------------------------------Worthless
Creative---------------------------------Inability to Do
Adequate--------------------------------Inadequate
Something-------------------------------Nothing
Oneness----------------------------------Being Alone
Wisdom----------------------------------No Wisdom
Truth--------------------------------------No Truth
Love---------------------------------------Loveless

The area of the Diamond of Awareness that deconstructs the *trances* associated with I am are quite extensive and are only limited by your questions. Being awake helps us to stay aware of whom we are. By balancing the interaction between the territory and the *mapping system*, we are able to be clear about whom we choose to be.

I Am, Here

The next section of The Diamond of Awareness deals with location. You are the location of awareness, and from this position, you locate yourself in space. Distance is measured from this position to all other objects or positions. The body is always here. It is never there. Within the Diamond of Awareness is the *here* and being here is what we can experience. Outside of the Diamond is the *there* and the there is not experienced, it is only imagined. Notice we can imagine being across the room, across the street, across town or the state but imagining is not the same as being there. We may even imagine being in a magical place or nowhere. We spend time making up or trying to figure out what is going on over there. Noticing what is going on with another person or object is projection or pure imagination. How often have you tried to think about what is happening somewhere else or what another individual is thinking feeling or experiencing only to find that you were entirely off in your story. Think about location. Where are you now, what room, what building, what town, what county, what state, what country, what continent, what hemisphere, what galaxy are we in.

I Am, Now

The next section of the Diamond of Awareness assists in the deconstruction of the *trances* around time. We experience ourselves as being in time or as going through time. Our sense of time is created internally, and then set on automatic so, it appears to function separately from us. The physical body is always present in the now. It is not found in the past or wandering around in the future. Consciousness reconstructs the past or projects the future over the present experience...

Time Lines

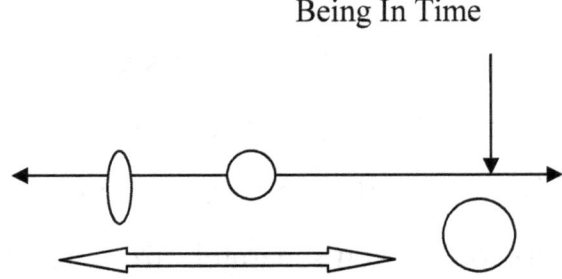

Being In Time

Going Through Time

People are aware of being present, fully being where they are, and enjoying the event they are engaged in as if time were fluid and flowing. People may experience themselves moving from event to event as if time was solid, fixed or frozen and they are moving through it.

Become aware of how you experience time. Does time seem to move slowly or does it move quickly depending on whether you are enjoying the experience or not? Experiences, identities, emotional states all have a beginning, a middle and end. Here are some questions to get you thinking about time.

Time Exercise

In relation to (love, loss, person, place, or experience)
  X what was?

In relation to (love, loss, person, place, or experience)
  X what is?
In relation to (love, loss, person, place, or experience)
  X what will be?

Also, ask
In relation to (love, loss, person, place, or experience)
X what was not?

In relation to (love, loss, person, place, or experience)
X what is not?

In relation to (love, loss, person, place, or experience)
X what will not be?

Another type of questioning regarding time, deals with the things that you assume, decide, or believe about objects, people, places, or things. Whenever a decision, assumption, belief, or philosophy comes up trace it to its origin or earliest remembrance.

Assume, Decide or Believe Exercise

Notice something that you assumed, decided, or believed and ask the following:

I know that when you were X years old, etc. - you assumed, decided or believed that then. Are you still assuming, deciding or believing that now, and if you can, notice who or what authority told you that?

Is there any associated judgment, preference or significance affecting the assumption, decision or belief and is there any interaction of the judgment, preference or significance?

An example of this would be as follows: *When Susan was 8 years old, she believed that her mother knew everything and could read her thoughts. Now that she is an adult of 25, she sometimes feels that she cannot hide things from her mother because of this old belief.* If she says that it is *good* that she tells her mother everything about her life, it is an effect of a judgment. Beliefs that we create in the past if not examined now in the light of present information, automatically popup and affect how we perceive things. Once a belief is formed, the original belief is the strongest and if it is followed by positive results, it will become part of the *mapping system*. If this interaction is repeated, its functioning may become automatic. A point of interest may be that energy is said to be neither created nor destroyed, it just changes form or is transmuted. Within the *neural information centers* are contained all references to known objects and within those centers and their interconnectedness are the rules for how they are associated or referenced. This is based on the idea that contained within the *sensory perceptive holographic mapping system* is not only the original object construct (representation) but also all references and history of varying associational linkages and their rules of acknowledgement, use and nonuse of the object. We consider that our personal or idiosyncratic interpretation of stimuli is dictated by the original representational object as modified by the association with all representational objects within that class or category. This would bring up some references to category and scope. Category is a designation of a certain set of similar objects, stimuli or experiences while the range, limit, and rules for inclusion or exclusion and there defined functions would be the indicators of scope. Category can also be used to indicate distinctions of classes that objects can be divided into.

Recognition of Present Time Stimulus, Objects, and Experiences

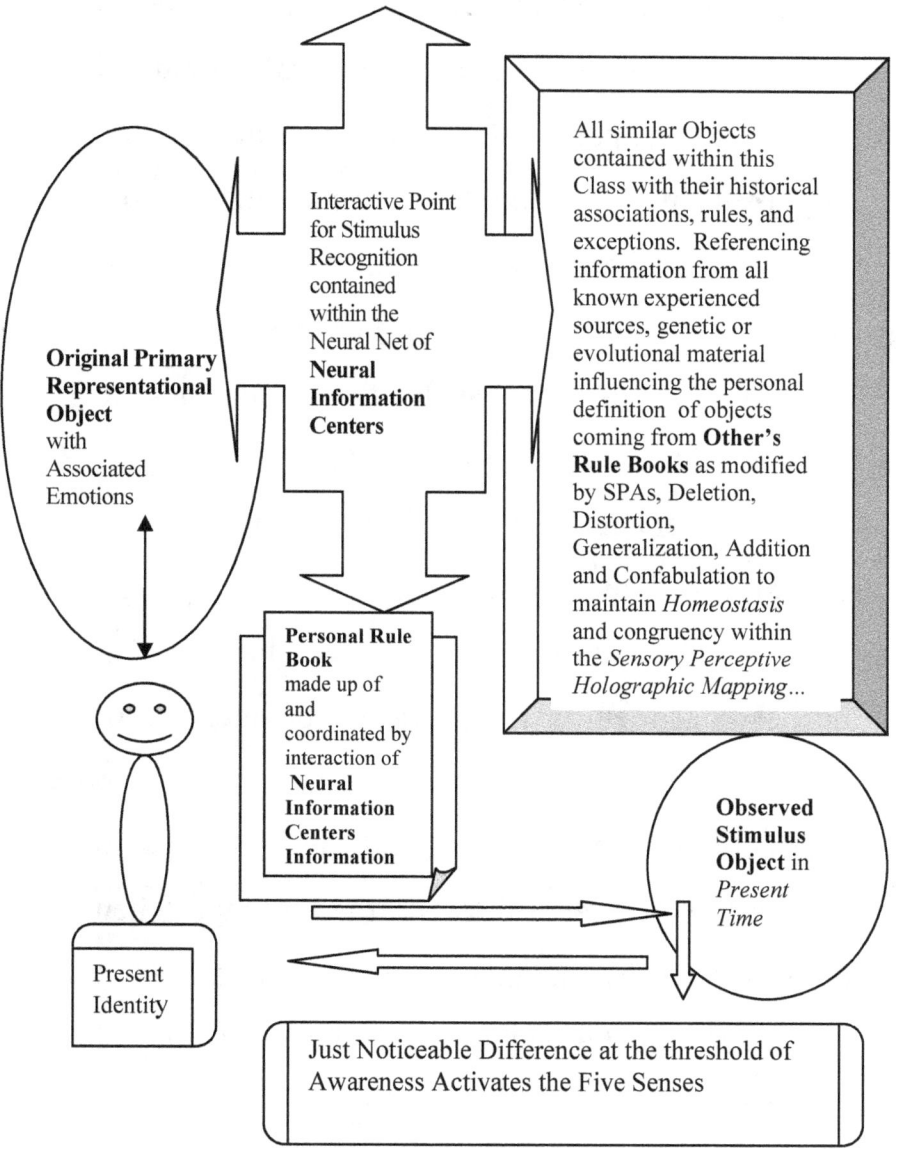

The genetic/evolutional need and survival indicators dictate or guide the original biological response to stimuli. Biological needs are safety, water, nutrition, comfort, attachment (merging), learning and information completion, which are all geared to the nervous system's primary focus of survival. The natural essential interaction with the environment and the energetic flow is interrupted and mediated by the *socialization* process of interaction with others. The rules and injunctions from others' interpretation (*others' rulebook*) of the world begin to be the foundation of our *personal rulebook* and the giving of judgments, preferences and significances in relation to need acquisition and behavior. The impact of others is a natural part of development, but it begins to compartmentalize the thinking, feeling, and responding of the organism into an unnatural responding to the environment self and others. An internal considering of internalized rules of interpretation and their judgments, preferences, significances and their interaction, interrupts the natural flow of response by the organism. So within the neural net is contained the original stimulus, all the biological indicators, the interpreted rules of others, and the organism's created rules of response. The conceptual world and the constructed rules overlays the natural biological interaction with the environment. Within the *mapping system*, the construct of the personal identity is created as an interface of interaction with the world. The survival mechanisms of the nervous system do not or cannot differentiate between the biological and the imagined, so any perceived threat to an identity is seen as a threat to the biology. Then we begin living in a world constructed by metaphors and interpretations of what the environment means or should be according to the mythological constructs of our family, group, culture and our biological progenitors. Within the messages of judgments, preferences and significances are the stories or rules (beliefs and philosophies) of how to survive better. The message is we need to learn these rules and apply them to living and that we need to or should know them. There are instances when a child makes errors and is told, *you do not know what you are doing, what were you thinking, you should know what to do, haven't we taught you anything.* The biological being is separated from the environment and looses its harmony with its essential self. Remember, *the spirit is willing, but the flesh is weak* is a message about the subjugation of the flesh and a judgment of its inherent weakness and badness. Within this rule is also the preference for the higher functioning spirit as opposed to the body thus separating the organism from itself. Since, we are told that we should know things (the rules) to survive; we have developed a biological learning response and a biological completing response (Gestalt closure). Therefore we should, *know, predict and control* in order to survive better. The organism's natural responses to danger are a search and scan mechanism along with the flight, fight, or freeze response. Since the nervous system can only respond to things it recognizes and knows, the things it is looking for have already happened and are in the past. Therefore, the nervous system is constantly projecting an overlay of the past over the present so it can survive in the future from events it has already survived. *Present time sensory awareness* creates a null set, or reset point to momentarily disrupt this mapping overlay of the present with the past. Therefore, enlightenment is a return to the natural connection of the environment (territory) and the biological self (self in territory). The biological being and the environment are one and are congruent when they interact and are not mediated by a conceptual, mythological world.

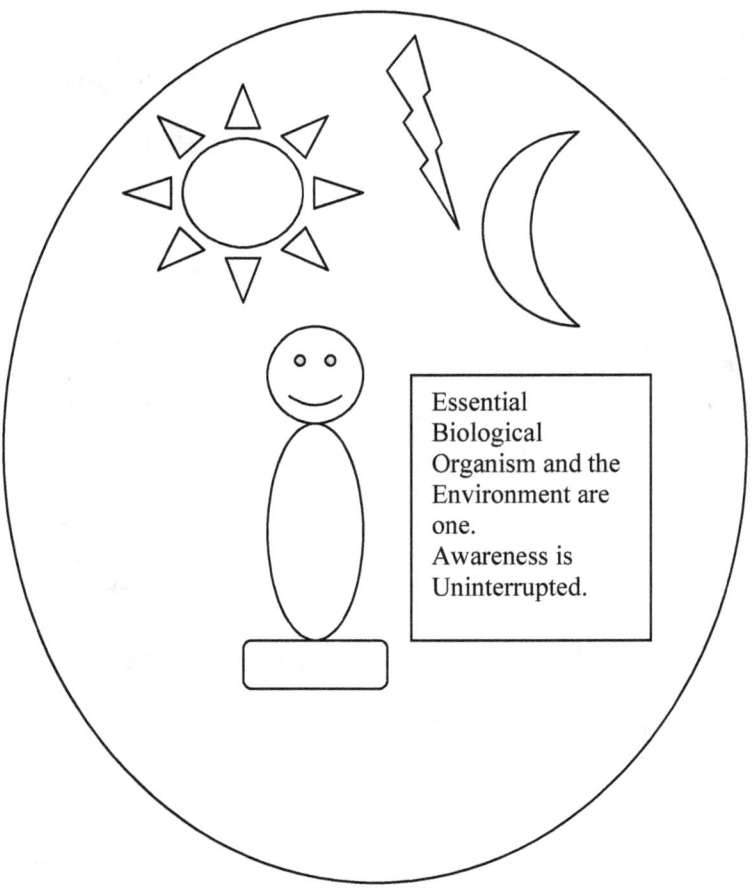

The Person and Environment as One

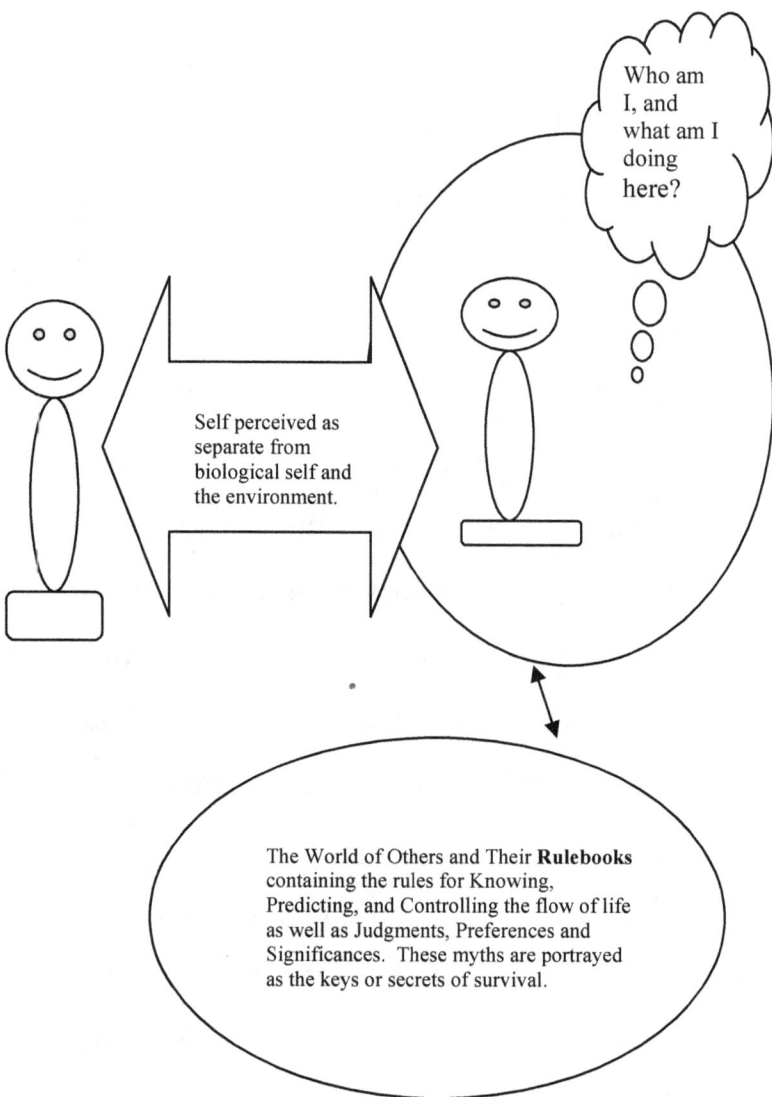

**Socialization and the Conceptual
World That Compartmentalizes and Separates**

Rulebook Metaphor

The rulebook is a metaphor for the *neural information centers* and their ability to acquire, categorize, respond to, and utilize stimuli (information). The Sensory Rulebooks may be similar to books in that they contain information but they are additionally multi sensory. They use all available senses to construct the sensory representations, their associated emotional states, and any accompanying editorial explanations. The representations can be various visual images, auditory sounds, dialogues, tactile sensations, smells, tastes; and they may contain access to a singular stimulus or a complex interconnection and interaction of sensory stimuli that construct a multi-sensory, multi-dimensional experience or memory. Within the *sensory mapping system* is a massive library complex that maintains a referencing system of all experiences and a history of experiences and their explanations from all known sources. The library complex is a way of describing the categorizing sensory information into the various classifications and subjects. The books separate sensory material into their designated areas and scope of reference. Although, not fixed there are rules of connection and categorization and usage that are both universal and idiosyncratic and made up by the nervous system.

Inherent Sensory Perceptive Mapping Errors

The Diamond of Awareness assists the user in remembering *to be aware* of the *Here* and *Now*. This is useful because the *mapping system* is always referencing the past. The nature of the biological system is to reference incoming sensory data to past objects, experiences and the associated emotional, energetic orientation toward that object. Thus, the images, sounds, and emotional orientation are experienced as if they are occurring now, but in fact, they are referencing objects, experiences, and emotions in the past. The *mapping system* is an abstracted representation of the territory as constructed within the nervous system. Survival and navigation through the territory are the goals of this representational hologram. Remind yourself that what is being experienced is always being filtered and altered by the *mapping system*. This is a continuous challenge. Remind yourself to be aware that the linking of present stimuli with past-created representations of similar stimuli creates a representational blend within the sensory *mapping system* and is not accurate. Distortions, deletions, generalizations additions, and confabulations (blending of stimuli, past, present, created, with their associated meanings, and emotional states) are the tools used by the nervous system to keep the *mapping system* congruent and maintain *homeostasis*. This is where s*ensory perceptive alteration* assists with the maintenance of internal and external stimuli referencing by altering sensory data and its integration into the ongoing storyline created by the nervous system through the lens of an identity.

The Diamond of

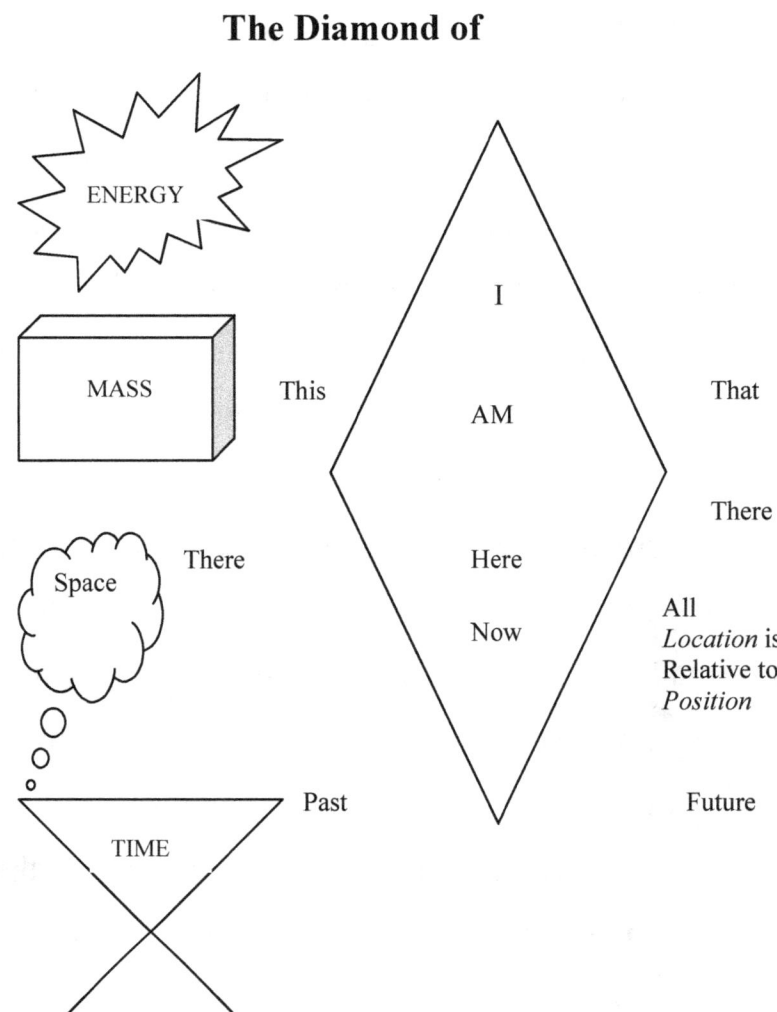

Awareness

Figure 4

The Diamond of Awareness is a method of increasing awareness of *present time sensory alignment* and disruption or interruptions of s*ensory perceptive alteration*s or *cognitive programming errors*. This particular way of working with the organism, was developed during studies with Dr. Stephen Wolinsky, the founder of the Quantum Psychology Institute. It is simply a method for increasing awareness of the focus of attention and the various underlying stories, beliefs, lies, and imaginings we call reality and life. The Diamond of Awareness can be used as a tool to be used for *enquiry*, that is to question and confront the concepts that are created. The Diamond can be used to assist with trance Deconstruction or interruption and the Diamond can be used in a similar way to the meditations dealing with the space between two (2) breaths to dissolve the experience.

Exercise

> *Sit comfortably and notice as a thought comes up or materializes. Ask yourself where does that thought come from. Then if you notice another thought, ask where does that thought come from. Do this with several thoughts. Pause*
>
> *As the thought goes away, ask yourself where does that thought go. Do this with several thoughts.*
>
> *Now notice that these thoughts come from the space and return to the space. This is a dissolving exercise; it helps you to notice the space.*
>
> *The Diamond of Awareness will also bring you back to the space.*

Each section of the Diamond is used to cut away the layers of illusion, programming errors, and *sensory perceptive alteration*s that distort or prevent the organism from more clearly experiencing reality. The center of the Diamond contains what "I" consider experience-able. The individual is encouraged to notice the "I am" without additions or subtractions from the *sensory mapping*. The "I" represents the conscious sense of presence. The "I am" is what is known. The "I am" *this* or *that* is what is created and generally comes from outside the experiencer's internal world. The "I am" a man, a woman, an American or any other descriptor such as likeable, ugly, stupid, smart etc. is what is created. It is also the foundation of identities or *SPA* states. Remember that "I" + anything (Statement) = an identity. When you begin to notice the body or physical organism, where do you experience or sense its location? It is usually experienced as *here*. The time you notice the physical form is always *now*. The experiencing of the physical body is always *here* and *now*, however the experience of the "mind" or conceptual person can be *here* or *there* and can be in the *past* or *future*. The mind has no location in time or space or so it imagines, so it can tell itself things about what may be occurring in other parts of a room, a city, a country or in distant galaxies. It "the mind" can make decisions about what other people feel, think or intend without bothering to question or confirm its accuracy. The mind can respond to things that are occurring in the present as if they are events that happened in the past. The mind predicts and anticipates the future as if it knows what will occur. As you, explore the world inside the diamond of awareness (I Am Here Now) notice that the area on the outside of the diamond is filled with things that are imagined. These things are interpreted to have meaning but those meanings are derived from associative and assumptive meanings. When the mind or "consciousness" asks a question and there is no answer, "consciousness" will answer itself. This is what we have called the completion or Gestalt closure error. In the absence of information, the mind will create its own and conveniently forget that it is the source. This is one of the reasons that our *sensory perceptive mapping* world is confabulatory and filled with distortions and misinformation. The use of the Diamond of Awareness simply increases awareness and frees consciousness to be present.

The Diamond of Awareness is to assist you in becoming more aware of the creations of the mind/body. It is like an iceberg that you have brought into the sun exposing more and more of what was below the surface to your awareness. Whatever you are doing unknowingly, unconsciously and unintentionally begin doing knowingly, consciously and intentionally. Most of us imagine that there is only one identity or observer but in fact, there are identities for each experience. There is an observer for each observation. Become aware that identities come and go. In fact, they appear and disappear. The nervous system resists the void, space or emptiness and the chaos of not knowing by creating. The mapping is an attempt to know, predict and control the flow of energy and the outcome.

Mapping construction, deconstruction, and reconstruction is a natural ongoing process of the nervous system. *Neural information centers* are the neuro-chemical imprinting or copying of the stimuli within the five senses. The associative, assumptive, and referential meanings are a neuro-chemical response to the stimuli as they are referenced within the *mapping system*. Meanings are created through interactive perceptions. The *mapping system* engages in a process through biology, *socialization* integration, and emotion that engages the multi sensorial and multi associational *mapping system* and it is balanced by *homeostasis*. When we observe and do not know, we create knowing through the Gestalt closure process. We select the meaning from what is already available in the *mapping system*. The *mapping system* assimilates and accommodates new experiences and attempts synthesis. The memory of pain creates fear and the memory of pleasure creates desire. The mapping system of the organism is continually learning. It merges and then detaches from various experiences and stimuli. There are times when this process is fused in the experience. Either fusion creates an agreement with what is experienced or there is a resistance. Confusion may occur during this experience. This confusion is the *fusion confusion illusion* where the identity we have taken on is believed to be who we are. This may happen when a child tries to help depressed parents by trying to take on the depression. The child then forgets taking it on and begins to think and feel it is their depression. We often take on the injunctions or descriptors given to us by parents, siblings, friends or teachers, forgetting that it is not who we are. We observe or interact with others such as (parents, siblings, friends, teachers, and authorities) and hear, see, feel the interactions and this is how we learn to get our needs met. We have biological needs such as those listed in Maslow's Hierarchy including food, shelter, safety, love, belonging and self-actualization. The areas that the nervous system through identities is engaged in are as follows:

Developmental Areas of Focus

Safety
Needs
Boundaries
Esteem
Will (freedom)
Love/Sex/Competition
Sexual/Asexual

Dichotomy

Presence--- ---------Absence
Needs-----------Other's needs
Autonomy ----------Enmeshment
Grandiose----------Worthless
Control---------------Controlled
Sexual----------------Asexual

In an attempt to find ourselves, we look outside of ourselves for the answer and get lost. The primary loss is the betrayal and loss of self to get something. In an attempt to find ourselves we create an image and pretend it is who we are, there is effort to maintain the identity but then we become fearful thinking it may be false and we create a new identity? Identities appear spontaneously in response to stimuli. By focusing inside, we loose contact with the external territory, by focusing externally we loose perception of our internal state. A balancing between the external territory and our internal map is necessary for accurate perception. Awareness of these factors is useful in creating a bridge between the two.

Energy, Space, Mass and Time

All things in the known universe have the qualities of energy, space, mass and time. Energy is noticed in the strength, intensity, or movement of things whether they are thoughts, emotions, elements, or objects.

Space is all around and it is measured in distances close or far. All things require space to occupy.

Mass can be heaviness, lightness, ethereal or dense. Mass can occupy great areas of space or be very dense and take up very little area.

Time moves quickly or slowly and measures all things.

Notice how things have movement, or are they frozen? Is the movement fast, or slow? What about the intensity. Where do things appear, and what is their location? What is the duration of the object or experience? Who decides what it means?

Location Exercise

Notice how you locate yourself. (Name, family, or city)

Who are you? (Name, sex, race, religion, or role)

Where are you? (Location)

When are you? (Past, present, or future)

Create an identity, feeling or experience.

Step into the experience, now step out of the experience.
Step back in the experience. Pretend that it is you.

Pretend that you are, not pretending. Now let the experience dissolve.

What observer observes that?

What experiencer experiences that?

What decider decides that?

What believer believes that?

Now, turn your attention around and notice what if anything did all of that?

The organism develops a survival response, which is called the fight, flight freeze response, with it there is a scanning and search response that assist with the survival response. Subcategories of the survival response include a learning response and a completion response. We resist not knowing and being out of control by developing the knowing, predicting and controlling response. There are infinite positions or frames through which to experience life. The Diamond of Awareness assists you in loosening associations and frames so you can expand awareness, increase experience, and offer choice.

Identity Exercise:

When you step into an identity, ask yourself the following questions.

What are you doing?
Who or what are you being?

What are you, having?

What are you creating?

What are you expecting?

Who or what are you resisting? In addition, consider,

Who or what are you not doing, not being, not having, not creating, not expecting, and not resisting?

You need to be aware of the combinations, permutations, transmutations, and conditioning of identities.

There are *mapping errors* where there is misinformation within the *mapping system* itself. There are *mapping misapplications*, which is when a map is used in an incorrect situation or in a time or location where it does not apply. Then there are m*apping transpositions*, which is when one map is placed over another map as if it was not there or did not matter.

Life on Life's Terms

No matter what happens, keep your feet moving."
Bill O'Hanolin, (Training Seminar 1983)

"If what you're doing isn't working, do something else."
R. Reid Wilson, Ph.D., (One-Year Training Program in Strategic Psychotherapy and Clinical Hypnosis 1986)

People often become confused between life and their stories about life. All of us would certainly like to have things our way all the time, but we learn through the years of experience that we do not always get what we want. However, as Mick Jagger sings, "If you try sometime, you just might find, you get what you need..." Moreover, even that may not be true. Life is not like the advertisement at Burger King, "Have It Your Way." Life is lived on life's terms, and things unfold the way they do. If you have many expectations, then you may experience disappointments and resentments. You may find yourself spending time trying to beg, negotiate, or force the territory to conform to your "map," "story," or "picture" of the world. This struggle is futile and is what we call incongruence. If you can function in the present and become aware of more accurate, sensory information, you may find yourself coming to *acceptance* of things as they are. This does not mean that you like or agree with things as they are. It simply means you are aware of things, as they are, not filtered through some illusion or story of how things *should* be. Those are the things we term myths, stories, and lies, based on programming, programming errors and *sensory perceptive alteration*s within the *sensory perceptive holographic mapping system.* Acceptance leads to greater congruence with the territory, and therefore may lead to decisions that are based on the territory, not on a story or fabrication.

There may or may not be structure to reality, however, the nervous system through the *sensory perceptive holographic mapping system* imposes a structure, so it can know, predict and control the outcome and survive better, or so it believes. We live in a conceptual world created by the nervous system through its symbols of words, images, sounds, and sensations.

"You have invented words like effort, inner, outer, self, etc. and seek to impose them on reality. Things happen to be as they are, but we want to build them into a pattern laid down by the structure of our language. So strong is this habit that we tend to deny reality to what cannot be verbalized. We just refuse to see that words are mere symbols, related by convention and habit to repeated experiences." (*I Am That*, 1973, Sri Nisargadatta Maharaj).

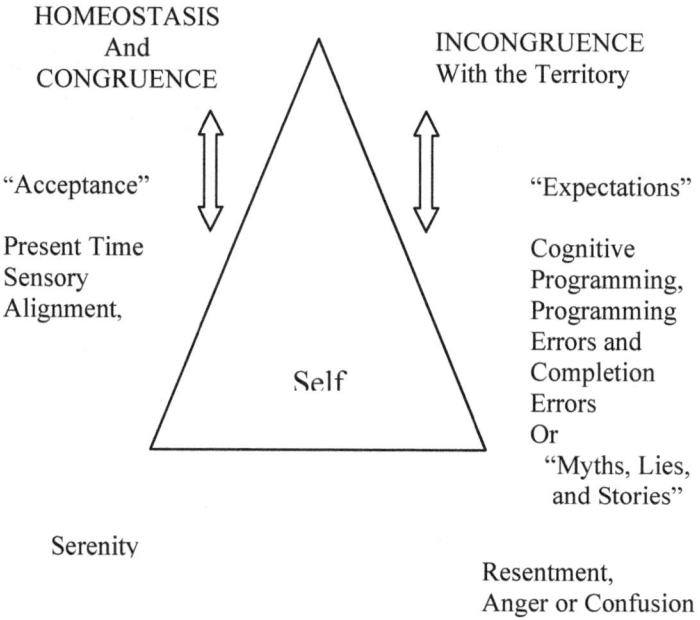

Figure 5: This illustration is an outlined approach for dealing with the energy or events of life on life's terms. Acceptance does not mean that we must like or agree with what is occurring. It means that we come into alignment with sensory information without extra distortions.

Resentment, anger, and confusion are the fruits from the seeds of "expectations" or *cognitive programming errors*, which we impose over the world.

ACCEPTANCE AND ALIGNMENT WITH THE TERRITORY

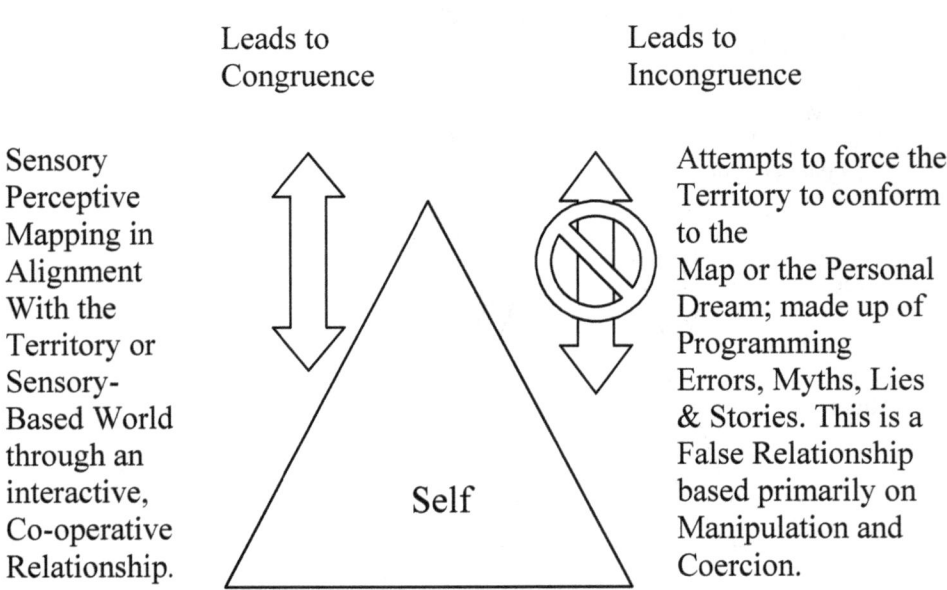

Figure 6: This illustration represents errors which move awareness away from sensory-based reality and toward the internally generated error laden *mapping.* Errors within the *mapping system* indicate that the representation of stimuli is influenced and altered by pre-existing programming, *cognitive programming errors* or s*ensory perceptive alteration*s rather than p*resent time sensory alignment.*

Trance Interruption Techniques

The following techniques are not to be used as a "how to" or as a "cookbook.". Work within the limits of your training, education and expertise. Best practice principles need to be applied.

Technique No.1
Present Time Sensory Perceptive Alignment:

Step 1. Ask the client to gaze at some object, which has neutral association for him or her.

Step 2. Sit or lie comfortably.

Step 3. Describe to yourself what it feels likes to position yourself in the seat, chair, or bed. For example, I can feel my entire body sinking into the fabric of the chair. I can feel my left foot (sensing) it feels heavier than my right foot. My muscles are beginning to feel limp. My breathing is beginning to slow and is now deeper in my chest.

Step 4. Take three deeper than normal breaths – slow, deep breaths, and upon each breath think to yourself R-E-L-A-X, allowing the air to slowly, leak out with each exhalation.

Step 5. You can allow your eyes to close. However; you can be in a deep comfortable state with your eyes open or closed.

Self-Pacing

Step 6. Try to hear and become aware of as many elements (sounds) in the environment as possible.

Step 7. Allow the sounds to be linked by the centers with images. Allow any images to be linked with the sounds. Allow any thoughts of the past or the future to be redirected back to the present streaming of thoughts.

Step 8. Now allow your thoughts to be projected onto a screen that you visualize out in front of you, about ten feet away and slightly above eye level. The screen becomes the channel through which and by which thoughts are conducted. Sound thoughts are even heard as running through the screen display.

Step 9. Now give your n*eural information centers* permission to operate independently performing the following:

> (b) Redirect all thought to the present time (no past or... future thoughts).
>
> (I) Start one center counting down from 1000 to 0 by 1's.
>
> (II) Start another center counting from one to 1000.
>
> (III) Have another center send commands to the body to "be calm – relax."
>
> (IV) Have yet another center narrate and create healthy body state.

Step 10. Remind yourself if you start feeling overwhelmed to let go and allow the centers to do their work. A center can check in from time to time on it's status, but let them do their work. Trust the centers.

Step 11. Continue to allow the centers to develop their autonomy.

Step 12. Recognize any source of tension in the body and request that the center in charge provide "release and relaxation."

Step 13. Allow the steps above to become a more fluid and flexible schema under the direction of the *homeostatic* system, rather than a rigid schema. Remember the *homeostatic* system is seeking balance and congruency.

Step 14. Count from one to five when signaled by a *neural information center* to do so. Allow your eyes to open, and be fully alert and present.

Technique No. 2
Dislocation Trance:

Step 1.   Begin by shaking off any tension in your arms, legs, neck, or shoulders, and be here with me now.

Step 2   Generate the *present time sensory alignment* state from the previous exercise (Steps 1 through 12). When you are fully relaxed, ask a center to give you a special place or a series of places that you can go.

Step 3.   When you have an image of a place, move into the image. Look to your right, look to your left, and now in an internal way describe to yourself what you see. Allow yourself to see, hear, and feel the textures. Notice the contrast of dark and light and any other variations in the scene. Feel your movement and rhythm as you move through the scene, and allow yourself to notice or become aware of any scents or smells.

Step 4.   Expect the experience to unfold through the associated links of the *neural information centers*.

Step 5.   Allow the outside world to fade as you experience this new state of awareness or *trance*. (*sensory perceptive alteration* state*)*

Step 6.   If you drift away from your pleasant scene, allow the *neural information centers* in charge to redirect you back into the description and experience of the scene.

Step 7.   Count from one to 10 and experience the present time sensory state with eyes open. Describe the surroundings to yourself and re-ground. For example, "I am sitting in the chair and I can feel the fabric of the chair. I can see a desk, bookshelf, and a window. I hear the heating/air conditioning system operating."

**Technique No. 3:
Connecting With Your Centers**

Introducing yourself to neural information center work.

Step 1.   Close your eyes and pace with yourself, (I am sitting in the chair, I am taking relaxing breaths. I can feel a tingling in my right foot. My left foot feels heavier than my right or vice versa. I can feel my back sinking into the chair.)

Step 2. Allow a center to direct you to your right or left hand by initiating a question "which hand?" and then accepting a signal. The signal can be any type of sensation.

Step 3. Thank the center for the communication.

Step 4. Ask the right (or left) hand center to communicate with you and give you a signal that it will work with you by signaling through one of your fingers (ideomotor). Creating a small level of movement in one of your fingers is requested. This signaling consists of one (1) movement for "yes" and two (2) movements for "no."

Step 5. If a "yes" signal is given, ask the hand center to connect with any other centers necessary to change the sensation in the selected hand. Ask the center. "If you are willing or ready to change the sensation in the right (or left) hand, let me know by giving me a signal. One X for "yes" or two Xs for "no."

Step 6. If "yes" signal is given, ask the center to start at the tips of the fingers and very gradually moving back, make the hand more like a cloud hand (light, fluffy, floating), a shell of a mannequin hand, or more not there than there. Ask the center to connect with any other centers or resources that it may need to create the change.

Step 7. If the answer is "no," move to the next paradigm (*Homeostatic System Check*). The no indicates that some other centers need to be consulted, or resources are not present within the system to establish the request.

Technique No. 4:
Homeostatic System Check: (HSC)

Step 1. Access a *neural information center* simply by making the request "I would like to be in communication with the center in control, responsible for, or having the information regarding (subject of inquiry)." (This could be right hand, left hand, or a sensation such as butterflies in the stomach, etc.).

Step 2: Ask, would you be willing to give me some information about the change to be made or history of the problem? Give a signal, one movement for 'yes' and two movements for 'no' (Most frequently, especially when requested, this will be an ideomotor signal. However, we respect the idiosyncratic nature of the system and will accept any signal.)

Step 3. If the answer is "yes" (usual occurrence), proceed to step 4-5. If the answer is "no," then ask the center to give more information about "What would be necessary to have such information?"

Step 4. Ask the center to search the system and recruit any centers for necessary information and resources addressing the desired change or problem.

Step: 5. Ask the center to give you a definite signal when the task is completed.

Step 6. Ask the center to arrange the following:

- (a) To give information about the problem or change requested (Be prepared to accept visual or auditory messages.)

- (b) Ask if the change or the problem can be safely addressed, "yes" or "no" answer (Wait for signal.)

- (c) If the answer is "yes," then ask the center to go inside and connect with all centers necessary to make this shift.

- (d) Ask the center when this connection has been made.

- (e) When signaled, ask the center to show or tell you the option(s) you have available.

- (f) If option(s) is (are) clear, thank the centers for their work. Then instruct the centers to reconnect to make the change happen.

- (g) If the answer is "no" in step (b), then ask the center to signal "yes" or "no" (1X or 2X respectively) to the following queries:

    - (I) Can this change be made safely?

- (II) Do I have all of the resources available to me to make the change?

- (III) Is the time right to bring about this change?

- (IV) Is some part of the system in opposition?

(h) If the answer to I – IV is "no," then ask the center to go inside and connect with any and all centers to access more information to illuminate what elements are necessary to bring about this change. Ask the center to signal when you have information.

(i) When signaled, thank the centers for their cooperation. Then ask them to show or tell you what elements are necessary to lay a foundation for future change or resolution.

(j) If the answer to IV was "yes," then proceed with the following:

- (I) Ask the center if it will contact the opposing center (one signal for "yes" and two signals for "no").

- (II) If "yes," thank the center and ask it to connect with the opposing center.

- (II) Ask the opposing center if it will speak with you (one signal "yes" and two signals "no").

- (IV) If the answer is "yes," thank the center and explain that you understand that it is trying to assist the system by doing its part. Begin queries of "yes" or "no" of variety based on signal system. Ask the opposing center to work with the other centers to show you its point of view.

- (V) Use the information from above for resource building and acquisition of information to be used in an information update technique.

Technique No. 5
Neural Information Center Updates:

After conducting a *Homeostatic System Check*, an opposing center may be discovered whose opposition may be based on outdated information. This is a common occurrence for Cognitive Behavioral Therapy as illustrated by the following:

A young lady persisted in experiencing mild headaches and nausea, growing to near panic, on her morning drive to the office. This was despite the radical, positive change in her work environment. When challenged to log or record what she was telling herself, she revealed the following statements: "Here I go again… another bad day at the office. I hate the way I must live. Life sucks." Upon discussion of the reality of the changes, she agreed that the statements were not valid. Accurate statement replacements were made, such as, "That's the way things use to be, but not now. I now like my boss. I can easily get my work done and it is helpful to others."

The previous represents a more classic, Cognitive Behavioral Therapy process of thought replacement and cognitive restructuring, utilizing the neural information concept for cognitive restructuring, *trance* deconstruction and replacement. The model for the same issue would be as follows:

Step 1: Access the *neural information center* associated with the symptom or issue (Frequently this will be the opposing part discovered through the *Homeostatic System Check.)*

Step 2: Thank the *neural information centers* for its communication with you.

Step 3: Move from "yes" or "no" signaling to the thoughts of a talking picture nature.

Step 4: Ask the center to convert pictures to thought of a word nature. (i.e. You see yourself in a bubble. What might you be telling yourself in that bubble? What word thoughts would replace the pictures?) What might other centers be saying about this picture? Pursue active dialogue with you and the centers. Put each word thought to the following test:

> a. Is this thought accurate with current or present time?
> b. Is this thought helping?
> c. Would I teach this to a child?
> d. Could I defend this thought based on facts?

Step 5: Replace word thought that not does meet the test.

Step 6: Ask the center to signal acceptance (yes or no) of thought.

Step 7: Ask the center to check throughout the system for acceptance or resistance to the new thought and signal "yes" or "no."

Step 8: If the center signals "no acceptance," then ask the center to give the reasons. Continue with updates based on new information, if necessary. Check again, and if the center stills signals "no," perform the *Homeostatic System Check*.

Step 9: If there are other centers resistant to the new thought, then (as above) request dialogue and begin any update necessary.

Technique No. 6:
Promoting Dialogue between Polarized Centers:.

Polarized centers are those *neural information centers* of which one is usually highly organized but seemingly encapsulated. These are revealed in the client's dialogue regarding his or her life with others. The following example illustrates this. Jane reports that prior to her first child, she frequently enjoyed sex with her husband, noting, "I would dress in my naughty lingerie and fantasize that I was a high paid call girl, but after I became a Mom and all, it just did not feel right. I would have sex with my husband to satisfy him and wait for it to be over. I don't know what happened."

Step 1. Establish two chairs or locations. (More may be used, if necessary.) Have available one tape recorder if desired.

Step 2. Place yourself in one position, and while sitting, "go inside and get in touch with one of the polarized centers" (in the previously proposed case the "Mom" center). Ask the center to begin to share with you information, memories, (visual and auditory, etc.) associated with the center. Allow this to continue until you "feel" emotional and/or physical changes.

Step 3. Experiment with pictures/thoughts/talk thoughts, bringing up colors, contrast, textures, pitches, volume. etc. that allow the center to disclose this position.

Step 4. When the feeling of this experience is "strong," count to 15 and rise from that position.

Step 5. Stand, engage in several deep breaths, and facilitate *present time sensory alignment*.

Step 6. When you are fully in present time and (only then) step into the opposing position.

Step 7. Repeat steps 2 through 4 again, this time working with this polarized *neural information center*.

Step 8. Stand. Again, reestablish *present time sensory alignment*.

Step 9. Still standing go inside and ask, "Which one" were you preferring to change Allow an exchange from the *neural information center* to guide you.

Step 10. Start the tape. Allow the *neural information center* to speak to its polarized counterpart. Give yourself time and permission to allow the *neural information center* to ask questions, chastise, communicate, discuss, etc. to the empty chair, which is the projection of its counterpart. When signaled by the appropriate n*eural information center* to change chairs or positions–do so. When reseated, allow that *neural information center* to respond, argue, vent, and communicate with its projected counterpart. Continue this interchange of positions and voicing or dialogue between counterparts until signaled by an executive *neural information center* which indicates, "It is time to stop." Please note that the *neural information center* executive may signal throughout this venture in a fashion very similar to what has been described as a "felt sense" (Gendlin).

Step 11. After the interchange has stopped, it will mean that the centers have become much more aligned and have begun to merge. To complete this merger, listen again to the tape, writing down indications of distortions held by each part. As the newly merged *neural information center* is operating, go inside and ask the merged center to work with other centers to give accurate updates or cognitions for each distortions or programming error noted on the tape.

Step 12. One by one, ask the merged centers, "Can you accept the new cognitions?" (Signal 1X for "yes" and 2X for "no.")

Step 13: Subject any "no's" to the *Homeostatic* System Check. Then again, ask the center if it can accept the cognition. At this point, the answer will frequently be "yes." If the answer is "no," query for any opposing center. Ask the center for its cooperation. (Signal 1X for "yes" & 2X for "no.") If "yes." begin dialogue with the center to update for change.

Technique No. 7:
Installation of New Auditory or Visual Messages:

Step 1. When installing an updated visual or auditory replacement message present the message, with these three tests."

 (a) Would you teach it to a child?

 (b) Would you advise your best friend to use it?

 (c) Would you be willing to defend it in court as fact?

If the message passes these three tests, then you can begin this installation.

Step 2. Have the *neural information center* in charge of visual messages begin with a dim, distant, colorless picture that incrementally increases in color, closeness, and intensity until it is a complete picture.

Step 3. If this is an auditory message, have the center in charge of the message begin with a soft message that increases with volume and intensity until it is a strong message.

Step 4: Once the message is at full intensity, check for any opposing centers.

TECHNIQUES TO STIMULATE THINKING METHODOLOGIES FOR INTERRUPTING PATHOLOGY OF THE CONSCIOUS SET

1. Trance Labeling

This type of technique gives us an opportunity to describe and interrupt the *trance* that takes us out of the here and now and distorts the experience by creating a confabulatory experience.

Throughout the day, we are engaged in any number of roles and/or activities, each of which can be labeled as a *trance* or altered state. When Susan is with her child Gregory, she can be in the "mommy" or "teacher" or "playmate" *trance*. When she is painting watercolors, she finds herself in the "artist" *trance* and when she is with her husband, she may be in the "partner," "friend," or "lover" *trance*. Some of the *trances* are specific and are reinforced by others and their expectations or the interactions we have with them, while some states of alteration have locations, times, duration, functions, and social meanings. Some of the alterations we experience are multifaceted and multilayered with other states of alteration. In other words, they may be state or context dependent or independent. Some alterations happen so frequently and may seem so natural that we barely notice them, if at all. While other alterations seem strange and awkward, there are altered states that we purposely create, such as meditation or acting in a play.

2. Video Camera

This particular intervention allows the individual to gain perspective by asking him or her to approach the scene, memory, experience as if viewing it through a video camera with the ability to change the view or the sound narration. When using this technique, ask the individual to notice anything that a mechanical recording device would not pick up and record.

This technique is an extension of a standard technique in the practice of Cognitive Therapy. The camera technique, in particular, is associated with Albert Ellis. However, extending this to the video camera, we are using it as a *trance* deconstruction mechanism. It is suggested to the client that in entering a situation in which he feels upset or inadequate, that the next time he begins to move into such an identified situation, to become a video camera. The video camera is to become one that is highly sophisticated. It sees nuances of shades or colors, can detect chemical compositions and report them as smell, and records a wide range of audio events. However, what it cannot record are emotions and descriptors of emotions. In essence, the video camera is a reductionistic mechanism that strips the client's interpretation of the event and reduces it to bare facts. This reduces the elements that are feeding into the dysfunctional *trance* and provides a means for *trance* shifting. The following is an example.

"John, I know that each time you go into your boss's office to ask for a raise, you start feeling like a small child, and you report feeling a great deal of discomfort in the pit of your stomach. You have reported to me that at the time you entered the boss's office, you began to make statements to yourself, such as, 'This is like it was back in the principal's office.' This is just like when I had to face my dad with a bad report card,' etc. You then have reported to me that your boss had an angry look on his face. You reported you saw the boss as growing larger, and you growing smaller. You reported that the room seemed very large, and you felt at a distance from it. For your homework, I want you to engage going into the boss's office. As you go into the boss's office, I want you to be the video camera. The video camera will see the doorframes, see the chairs, record colors, record shades within the room, and record high and low pitched voices. Being a sophisticated camera, it also will notice those chemical elements and identify smells. However, the camera will obviously not record anything that cannot be directly seen, heard, or sensed as a chemical element in the environment (such as taste or smell). Thus, the camera will not be recording such things that are non-existent to it, such as an angry posture of the boss, an angry look on the boss's face, scowling, a non-approving look, a large, threatening desk, etc."

"Now what I would like for you to do is to practice this technique in the park or at home. I would like you to feel free to have some fun with it. Become this video camera that is running reels, recording motions, recording action, but is not recording descriptors of any emotions nor making any guesses as to what any of the compilations of colors, movements, or gestures might mean."

3. Present Time Sensory Trance Alignment *(Reference to page 267)*

Present time sensory alignment is an intervention, which is described in detail on page 267.

4. Dislocation Trance/Noticing it as a Perpetuation of Trauma

Safe place teaching at will to create the changes. Notice when it is happening and give it a name. *(Reference to page 270)*

5. Diagramming the Trauma to include Sensory Representations

Diagramming the Trauma will also include associative meanings, referential and associational searches and the associated kinesthetics.

We can read a beautiful poem and experience sadness, anxiety, love, or hate because the power of the words with their associations on the paper begin to stir and connect with the associations within us and fire a complex chemical interaction of associations and firings which lead to emotions. However, if we take the same poem and we diagram it, we break it down to nouns, verbs, or gerunds, and we critically examine it for comma splices, run-on sentences, paragraph construction, etc., we begin to disrupt and destroy the meaning of the poem in terms of its *trance* effect or otherwise *sensory perceptive alteration* of it that has brought about these feelings. In other words, we destroy the art by disrupting the *trance* associated with the art in the same way as has been highlighted by workers in visualization, transformational grammar, and neuro-linguistic programming. It is possible to perform the same type of deconstruction technique with the *cognitive programming* that is running a trauma *trance*. The essence of this is that we actually ask the client to go inside and get in touch with the thought, to identify thought in the form of pictures, thought in the form of auditory experiences, and identify any associated physiological reactions in the body (nausea, tight muscles, headaches, flushing around the ears, etc.). We then painstakingly go back and have the client bring the trauma programming up. Systematically, we begin to analyze if there is a picture, then a sound, or if there is a sound and then a picture, and if the sequence initiates with a sound and then a physiological response followed by a visual response followed by a sound and a physiological response. In other words, we begin to make a recording of the chaining of thought, noting where in this chain a physiological response occurs. We graph this. We then have the individual go back and reconstruct the trauma based on the diagram, checking to see if we are getting the same physiological responses. Failing the same physiological responses, we then adjust our chain of events until we produce them (Caution: Sometimes, what happens is a deconstruction begins to occur when an individual becomes aware that his thought has such a chaining relationship and that this chaining relationship has a relationship to physiological responses). The individual is then instructed to draw a different diagram of the trauma experience using the diagrammatic elements previously recorded so that this time the sound might occur and then the picture, as opposed to the established, on-going sequence of the trauma chain, with the visual and then the sound. After a new sequencing is developed, the client is asked to follow the diagram and begin to run this newly constructed, programmatic chain in place of the old one. This is done three times. The client is then asked to produce further combinations of change within the programming chain, and this, too, is run three times. To address the physiological responses in the trauma chain, if an individual reports having a very tight chest, at the point in the diagram where this is indicated as a physiological response, the client is encouraged to take a very low, deep breath, hold it, and then gradually let this breath seep out. Another way of altering the physiological response is if the client is reporting tension in the back and neck, do some stretching exercises at this point in a trauma chain. By engaging in this, we begin to disrupt the underlying, *cognitive programming*, which disrupts the dysfunctional *trance*, and automatically a *trance* shift occurs.

6. Building a Congruent and Functional Present Time Trance

Building a congruent and functional present time *trance* based on the elements of *sensory mapping* and the sequencing of the elements within the trauma *trance*, we follow the diagramming sequence noted under "Diagramming Trauma," but in this sequence, we take the picture and sound elements as they were diagrammed initially, and we replace them with pictures and sounds that are occurring in the on-going environment. For instance, if in the face of the stimulus that provokes the trauma *trance* a picture first appeared, then in our newly developed schema we have a picture to appear of something in our current time—a lamp, couch, etc. If next a sound occurred in the diagramming of the trauma *trance*, we have a sound occur and note it in our present-time situation, such as the distant sound of the roadway, the distant sound of a washing machine, etc. If next followed with tightness in the stomach and chest, then in the present time we engage in taking slow, deep breaths as a replacement. In other words, we take the exact diagrammed sequence of *cognitive programming* whose changing leads to a dysfunctional *trance*. We use the diagrammatic elements (pictures, sounds, feelings, etc.), and we use these elements transposed into a present time sense to build a present time *trance* that is aligned with the here and now.

7. Screen (movie/video) Technique

This technique uses the metaphor of putting the images and sounds out in front of the visual field up on a movie screen.

This has been a technique that in various forms has been utilized by Shaman, hypno-analysts, NLP workers, and other workers in visualization. The client is asked to seat himself comfortably in a chair. Frequently as he is sitting there, we will initiate the technique of *present time sensory alignment,* although this is not mandatory. When we get the okay from the client that he is feeling comfortable, we ask the client to go inside and get in touch with a center or centers that can begin to project a TV screen ten to twelve feet away from the comfortable seating of the client. This can be framed with the client being in the room, or taken a step further, with the client seeing himself in a very comfortable, private, secure movie theater. When we secure the ideomotor signal from the center that it is willing to do this, we ask the center to go ahead and make the appropriate connections and to signal us again when the projection mechanism has been put in place. Upon receiving this designation from the center, we ask the client to go inside and get in touch with the center or centers that are the drivers, projectors, and initiators of the troubling thought, chain of thought, or experiences. When we receive an ideomotor signal from these centers that such contact has been made, we ask the centers if they will be willing to project the thought chain, whether sound or visual, as an experience coming from and around the movie screen. We emphasize to the centers a projection in which the experience is "out there." We then ask the individual to get in touch with other centers that allow the projection to be fast-forwarded, rewound, and allow the sound track to be speeded up or slowed down with the expected distortions. Securing this, we then begin to have the individual fast forward the troubling thought or chain of thoughts on the screen, becoming faster, faster, until the visuals turn into blurs and disappear from the screen. Any associated sounds or auditories become higher pitched, faster, and are reduced to high-pitched squealing and then disappear from the screen. We then ask the centers to do a rewind of the event that was projected. Thus, all the events, even to include the sounds, will take on the distortion of moving backward through space and time, accelerating rapidly in speed as they do so, until they become a blur and disappear from the screen. After training with this technique, the individual is asked to engage in the forward and rewind until the centers will no longer project the images on the screen.

For homework, the client is instructed that any time a stimulus triggers the centers firing this chaining or programming, immediately place this on the screen, and engage in the fast forward, and rewinding until the thought/chaining/programming chaining essentially is "burned out."

8. Identified Programming Errors *(See programming errors pages 79-91)*

9. Installation/Replacement

    a. Spoon feeding technique

    b. Internal replacement of resources with use of and direction by *neural information centers*. Ideomotor signaling may be utilized. (*Reference to page 280*)

10. Working with Polarized or non-Assimilated Information Centers *(Reference to page 278)*

11. Homeostatic System Check

We are seeking to come to a resolution between *neural information centers* that may be at odds and in conflict, rather than a disturbance of the *homeostatic* system at that point. (*Reference to page 272*) *also see Updating Centers page 276*).

12. Diamond of Awareness (*Reference to figure 4 on page 171*)

Method of p*resent time sensory alignment* that emphasizes (I Am Here Now).

This discards I am this or that; or I am there, not here; or I am in the past or future, and not now. Everything within the Diamond, such as I AM HERE NOW is seen as the known and experience-able while things on the outside of the Diamond are seen as the unknown, the created, fabricated, or abstracted requiring some alteration of sensory perception.

13. Life on Life's Terms *(Reference to figure 5 on page 183)*

Teaches the use of p*resent time sensory alignment* to deconstruct *cognitive programming errors*, confabulatory mapping, and completion errors when new experiences trigger pathological, *homeostatic* responses.

14. Use of Any Part of the Model

    (a)   *Homeostasis*

    (b)   *Neural Information Centers*

    (c)   *Sensory Perceptive Alterations*

    (d)   *Cognitive Programming Errors*

    (e)   *Sensory Perceptive Holographic Mapping*

    (f)   *Persistent patterns of Trance Clusters*

(g) *Semantic Reversal Mechanisms*
All elements and aspects of the model can be used separately or in relationships to initiate *trance* deconstruction.

15. Mind/Body Integration Interrogatory

What are you seeing? What are hearing? What are you feeling? Where are you experiencing that? Notice what physical space it is happening in, be it mind/body or somewhere else. This series of questions begins the focusing on the various interpretations that can occur. Dr. Wolinsky often offered many different techniques for working with energy or emotions (Personal Training, Wolinsky 1992). As you notice an emotion, also become aware of its location in the physical space of the mind/body. What is the emotion's size and/or what is the emotion's shape? Step into the space and notice what occurs. Step out of the space and notice what occurs. Notice the label you have given the space (such as anger, sadness, fear, etc.). Then peel back the label and notice what is behind or underneath the label. Keep experiencing and de-labeling the space until nothing else comes up. Then notice the energy, and let the energy do what the energy does. Other things to notice may be to expand and/or contract the space. Allow full experience of the energy and do not prematurely de-label. At any point, you can ask what observer observes that. Turn your attention around and ask, "What, if anything, has created all of that?"

16. Changing the Physical Aspects of the Identity

Changing posture, breathing, eye movements, and body positioning are all alterations of physical outward manifestations of internal experiences. Some disruption techniques of the outward manifestations of internal experience are as follows: So what does this mean? How do you experience this? When you become aware of your posture, breathing or gestures alter them, and notice what changes occur in your thinking and/or feeling. This is a very simple technique. It actually involves the client changing his posture, breathing, tension, and relaxation in his body by any means necessary that does not conform to the posture, stance, or breathing patterns that are witnessed during a period of being distressed.

John is afraid to disagree with anyone. He begins to have flashbacks of his father telling him he is never to speak back to him, and that he is disrespectful whenever he offers his opinion. He then has other flashbacks of college experiences when he was ridiculed for having ideas that were different from his peers. However, this *cognitive programming* is associated with posturing in which he literally slumps forward, crosses his arms across his chest, looks down, and develops a pattern of very shallow upper chest breathing. The client is asked to visualize himself approaching a conflict situation. As he does, the client is asked to take very low, slow, deep breaths, obviously in contrast to the upper chest, shallow breathing. The client is asked to pull his shoulders back until he feels them grounded against a chair or a wall. The client is asked to look up and look ahead, if not directly at the person, then looking to the side slightly. The client is asked to not only visualize this change in stance, but to physically adopt it as he is visualizing, approaching, and moving through the conflict situation. The client and the therapist next discuss the first signs of postural changes associated with this dysfunctional *trance* state. The client is instructed, "At the first indication of this postural change, then adopt the new scenario of postural changes that we have discussed." The client is given this as practice/homework over the next several days. The goal is that when the client begins to note the chaining of physiological responses developing, he disrupts them by engaging in the new chaining of behavior and thus begins to disrupt the old, dysfunctional *trance* in making way for the organism to replace it with a more functional *trance*.

17. "Ramana Maharshi Technique" *or* "Go Back the Way You Came"

There is a story that a person traveled a great distance to see the Hindu Saint, Ramana Maharshi. Because this person thought he did not know who he was, he felt that this caused him to suffer greatly, and he believed the saint could free him. When he arrived at the feet of Ramana, he said, "Tell me who I am" and Maharshi said, "Go back the way you came." The students of the guru were quite upset and questioned him, saying, "How could you be so cruel?" Maharshi responded, "No, you have misunderstood."

Follow the "I" thought back to where it arose. So when applying this type of questioning or enquiry you ask:

1. "Prior to this experience, what were the thoughts or feelings that were being experienced?" What was the state of the consciousness?

2. Prior to the event.

3. Prior to the trauma.

4. Prior to the belief.

5. Prior to the chaos.

6. Prior to being overwhelmed.

7. Prior to the body-mind.

8. Prior to the concept.

9. Prior to the identity.

10. Prior to the association.

11. Prior to the memory.

18. Neutral Filter

As you notice your focus of attention on some image, some sound, some feeling, some event, etc., ask yourself to become aware of any judgment, preference, or significance that is being associated with the focus of attention, and then remove it. Notice what, if anything, occurs. As you are working with individuals, become aware of any judgment, preference, or significance that comes up for you in relation to the person or his or her world. Remember that the changes and suggestions that occur need to be congruent within that person's universe, not yours, and he or she must live with the effects and impact, not you.

19. Wolinsky's Maneuver

Whatever you are doing <u>unknowingly, unconsciously, and unintentionally,</u> **now,** <u>do knowingly, intentionally, and consciously.</u> Often our patterns of thinking, feeling and responding become automatic or fixed. This procedure has us take things off automatic and notice who, what, when, where and how decisions and responses are made. We can then become aware of the steps to making the decision and re-decide whether it is still workable, now.

20. Schreiber/Hellams Mapping Paradox

Since all maps, concepts, and beliefs are abstractions, and all languages are symbolic representations of abstractions, we are not attempting to develop a rigid structure or suggest that this is the way. According to the Quantum physicists, all location is relative to position. All positions begin with an "I." Notice that whatever you read or contemplate is just a position that is abstracted from some "I." All of the contemplations are adjustments to the "I" concepts. Become aware of what "I" is affected by, the thought, belief, or idea. Without an "I," there is no map. All maps are "I" generated.

21. Wolinsky Step #2

As you allow yourself to step back to observe the identity, belief, etc., ask yourself', what observer is observing that and what, if anything, created all of that?"

22. The One Question

The singular question is who or what are you being or imagining that you are? From this question proceeds all other identity questions and their functions and purposes or goals. Below are a series of questions that can be asked.

Who or what do you imagine/think/feel/believe that you are? By being that, what, if anything, is wanted? What if anything is not wanted? If that were to occur, what would happen? What would not happen? What or who is being or not being resisted? Who or what authority told you to be that, or told you that, that would happen, or what the result or outcome would be?

Trance deconstruction and reconstruction is an ongoing process. It can occur on its own, or be initiated by the person exploring ways to make changes. Any aspect of energy, space-time, or mass can be altered; and sensory data or its perception may be altered to bring about trance deconstruction. Keep in mind that when there is any change in the Sensory Perceptive Holographic Mapping, then homeostasis will challenge the change, even if it is for the good of the organism. All of these shifts in focus may give one the opportunity to observe/experience the transmutation of identities and energy. In addition, the experience may loosen your trances/associations/references and frames of reference. Where you can, step in the experience, then step out of the experience, allow the experience to dissolve, and then remember, remain prior to your creations and experiences. You are there before the experience.

Installation/Replacement
Spoon-Feeding

1. When a client has difficulty deriving suitable thought replacement, therapist suggests possible replacement.

2. Therapist asks client to "go inside and connect with a *neural information center* that will help us."

3. Therapist asks the center to signal when it can hear the therapist. (This is usually a ideomotor signal.)

4. Once signal is received, center is asked, "Will you assist us in replacing _____ (the old thought) with _____ (the new thought). Lift one finger for "yes" and two fingers for "no."

5. If answer is "yes," use the model for *Homeostatic System Check* to replace thought, like replacing a behavior.

6. If answer is "no," then proceed to Internal Replacement.

Internal Replacement

1. Therapist asks client to "go inside and connect with a *neural information center*."

2. Therapist asks center to "signal if it can hear therapist."

3. Therapist presents center with thought that is a *cognitive programming error*.

4. Therapist asks, "Please work with any and all necessary centers to find a replacement."

5. Therapist asks center, "Please signal us when this has been accomplished."

6. When signal is received, therapist asks client to reveal new message.

7. Both apply "test" for appropriate programming (Programming Error Test).

8. If test is passed, therapist utilizes *Homeostatic System Check* with client to complete installation.

9. If "test" is not passed, client and therapist discuss implications for system's approval of a programming error.

The Flame and Light of Consciousness

With the combination of elements and the interaction of forces, the consciousness arises. The consciousness is neither the organism nor the environment it interacts with, but of which it is a part. The organism breathes, consumes, and transmutes the chemicals of the environment interacting with, assimilating, and changing them. That which appears infinite, unchangeable, and permanent becomes that which appears finite, changeable, and impermanent. As Buddha has stated Nirvana is Samsara and Samsara is Nirvana, this is, in fact, a description, a concept and an abstracted representation of the one substance.

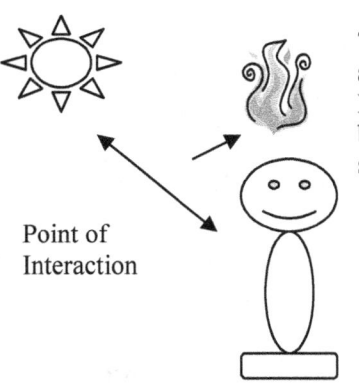

Point of Interaction

The Flame of Consciousness arises and subsides. It is the Body, it is the Infinite, it is both and neither. It is something in between.

The Infinite and the Finite are one. It is an illusion that they are separate.

The body appears to be, and yet it is not. Its appearance creates the illusion of presence and continuance when there is neither. The eight negations of Nagarjuna are an excellent explanation for the consciousness and its illusions.

> 1. Nothing arises, nothing is created, and nothing is born.
> 2. Nothing subsides, nothing is eliminated, and nothing dies.
> 3. Nothing ceases to exist, or can be destroyed.
> 4. There is no beginning, there is no end.
> 5. Nothing is the same as anything else, there is no unity.
> 6. Nothing is different from anything else, no duality.
> 7. Nothing arises, or comes.
> 8. Nothing subsides, leaves, departs, or goes.

Sri Nisargadatta Maharaj said to Stephen Wolinsky, "There is no birth, there is no death. There is no person. It is all a concept. It is all an illusion.

The flame of consciousness is a biological process that illuminates and projects images, shapes, and names onto the canvas of the void. It is "Maya" the great illusion of the "I" and its universe. In the Quantum world, the universe and the "I" blink in and out of existence 14 times a second.

I call this capacity for entering other focal points of consciousness-- love; you may give it any name you like. Love says; 'I am everything'. Wisdom says; 'I am nothing'. Between these two, my life flows (I Am That, Sri Nisargadatta Maharaj, 1973).

Is there a world outside of your knowledge? Can you go beyond what you know? You may postulate a world beyond the mind, but it will remain a concept, unproved and un-provable. Your experience is your proof, and it is valid for you only. Who else can have your experience, when the other person is only as real as he appears in your experience? (I Am That, Sri Nisargadatta Maharaj, 1973).

For Therapist

Assessment of client Request:

1. Is there a client?
2. Who or what is that client?
3. Is the client, the individual in front of you, some agency (social or private), or some other person?
4. What is the problem or request?
5. How is it a problem for them?
6. In what way have they attempted to resolve it is the past?
7. What is wanted from you?
8. How will they/you know when they have what they want or need?
9. Where will it be needed or used?
10. Who is in charge of its use?
11. Can it be described using the senses?
12. Use scaling questions where possible? from 0-10
13. Use the magical question when appropriate. *"If tomorrow when you wake up the problem or request you are making is resolved or fulfilled how would things in your world be different?*
14. How is the problem, dilemma, request and the solution represented in the client's sensory perceptive mapping system?
15. Calibrate to client's representational/sensory preferences. How do they *access*, *validate* and *represent* the problem/solution? Remember some representations are out of awareness.
16. Visuals, Auditory, Tactile, Kinesthetics, Olfactory, Gustatory and related schemas, cognitions, and Sub modalities.

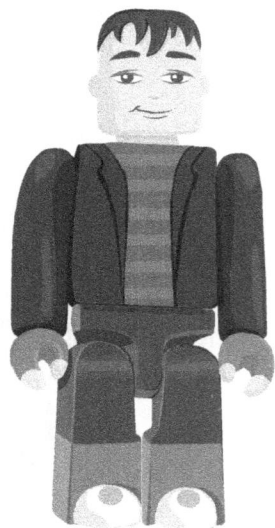

17. What is occurring and how is the problem and solution experienced and represented in Energy, Mass and Space-Time?

Energy= weak vs. strong, fast –slow

Mass= dense-light, heavy-light

Space-Time= distance, location, and position. Past, present, future

18. Past, present and future representation? In relation to this problem X what was? What is? What will be? Also include the opposite. In relation to the problem X what was not? What is not? What will not be?
19. How does the client experience time and code time? Do they experience themselves in time or going through time?

Past  Future

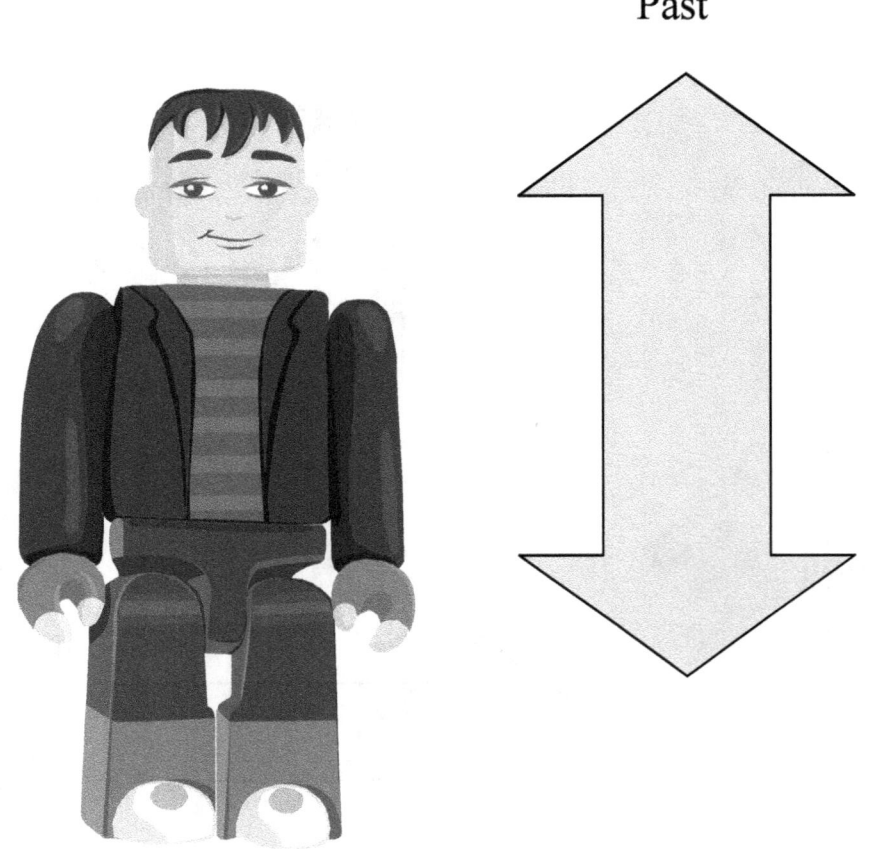

20. Sorting and coding time can be done in several different ways. Knowing if time is sequential or some other frame can be helpful.
21. Is there well formedness to the solution or goal? 1. Stated positively 2. Initiated and maintained by the person 3. Described in a sensorial way 4. Ecologically sound and Homeostatic.
22. Use of and Experimental stance? There are no mistakes only opportunities to learn. Who, what, when; where, and how?
23. What are you willing to know, feel, and experience?
24. What are you unwilling to know, feel, or experience?
25. What are deciding to know, feel, and experience?

The map is not the territory, but some relation between the territory and the map representation is essential. People function out of their representations not the senses themselves. To some degree life is a *"functional fiction"*, and as such the person is the creator of the drama.

Noticing the distortions, deletions, generalizations, additions, confabulations and gestalts gives guidance to the direction for giving greater congruence between the territory and the map. Whatever you are doing *unknowingly, unintentionally, and unconsciously*, do it *knowingly, intentionally, and consciously*.

Conceptualize the problem, challenge and the solution or outcome;

Choose a strategy, simplify the challenge, be specific, work in the present (here & now), be active, if what you're doing isn't working do something else.

Choose a method of implementation/ trance deconstruction. Remember, as Erickson said, "Depotentiate the conscious set".

Chunk the work into manageable pieces/segments. It is easiest to ride the horse in the direction it is going. Go for the point of least resistance.

Assess the results. Make sure all parts of the client are in congruence. Ask the client.

Is there any part of you that has concerns or is in disagreement with the solution or the effects?

> TOTE: Test, operate, test, exit. Start with the present position and aim for the desired position. This also refers to state change moving from Present state to the desired state.

Ways of Intervention:

Front Door: linear logic/ focus of change cognitive

Cognitive awareness

Lecture, education, information

Direct advice

Support –Rogerian

Rational-emotive challenge –ABC- irrational logic

Content interpretation (psychoanalytic)

"be here now" Gestalt

Awareness exercises

Analyzing games, transactions, scripts (T.A.)

Enhance self-disclosure and self-examination (client centered)

Developing the Observer

Side Door: analogy/ focus of change affective

Successive approximations or shaping procedure (behavior therapy)

Self efficacy-(Bandura) what best serves the self

Modeling

Transference issues

Free associations

Dream work

Guided fantasies

Empty chair (Gestalt)

Redecision (Gouldings)

Ego State parent-adult-child (TA)

Therapy relationship as proto type Microcosm

Instructions on peripheral behavior

Stories/metaphors

Collapsing anchors (NLP)

Emotional de-labeling (Quantum Psychology) Wolinsky

Swish Techniques (NLP)

Fast Phobia Cure (NLP)

Back Door: paradox/ focus of change behavioral

Flooding (behavior therapy)

Paradoxical Intention (Frankel)

Role-play polarities (Gestalt)

Exaggeration rituals (of the symptoms of resistance0

Prescription of symptoms

Relapse prescription – benevolent

Providing a worse alternative

Symptom substitution

Ambiguous function assignments

Skepticism re: desire or permanence of change

Pattern disruption: listed below

PATTERN DISRUPTION:

There is no fundamental reality."
Buddha

"It is all a play of perceptions and concepts."
Stephen Wolinsky

The use of interruption techniques can change the types of stimulus patterns within the *sensory perceptive mapping system*. Sometimes associations inhibit the ability to learn and to expand your awareness. Here are some methods for loosening association at those times when you might choose to loosen them. As you become aware of your *sensory perceptive holographic mapping system*, you can become more familiar with its editing functions and abilities. Within the *mapping system*, there are many areas that you can observe and adjust. In the sensory arena, there are visual, auditory, tactile, gustatory, and olfactory dimensions. Some descriptors that apply to each of these sensory areas are as follows: visual, [*color/black and white, brightness, contrast, focus, texture, detail, size, distance, shape, border, location, movement within the image, of the image, orientation, associated/dissociated, perspective, proportion, dimension, singular/plural*], auditory [*location, pitch, tonality, melody, inflection, volume, tempo, rhythm, duration, mono/stereo*], and kinesthetic [*quality, intensity, location, movement, direction, speed, duration*]. You can adjust the kinesthetic responses and the associated and referential meanings. In each of these dimensions, these descriptors can be edited, and the effects observed. The *sensory mapping system* can be treated as an object, and it and its contents can be observed. In the old school, this would be called "observing ego." Sensory data, energy, mass, and space-time can be observed, and their functions and effects can be altered. Using the pattern, interruption "map" it is suggested that you can vary the following elements:

1. *Change the frequency/rate of the pattern.*

2. *Change the intensity of the pattern.*

3. *Change the duration of the pattern.*

4. *Change the time (hour, day, week, and month) of the pattern.*

5. *Change the location (in the body and in the world) of the pattern.*

6. *Change some quality of the pattern.*
7. *Perform the symptom without the pattern.*

8. *Perform the pattern without the symptom.*

9. *Change the sequence of the elements of the pattern.*

10. *Interrupt or otherwise prevent the patterns from occurring.*

11. *Add (at least) one or subtract (at least) one new element to the pattern.*

12. *Break up any previously whole element into smaller elements.*

13. *Link the symptom/pattern to another symptom/pattern.*

14. *Reverse the pattern (O'Hanlon, William H. 1987. <u>Taproots</u>, Bruner/Mazel, New York).*

In energy, mass and space-time, there are qualities that can be observed. Energy can be observed as strong, weak, fast, slow, intense, or mild. Mass can be observed as weight, density, size, and shape. Space can be observed as distance, location, position, empty, full, infinite, figure, or ground. Time can be defined as movement, speed, duration, or direction. All of these elements of the s*ensory mapping system* can be observed, experienced, and altered, and the effects noticed. The movement of the eyes can be one method to assist in loosening associations. Think of a word, image, or sensation that has a positive association for you. Notice the location of the feelings. Now as you listen to the words visualize the image or feel the sensation. Follow these arrows with your eyes. This can also be used with uncomfortable or negative associations or simply associations you wish to loosen.

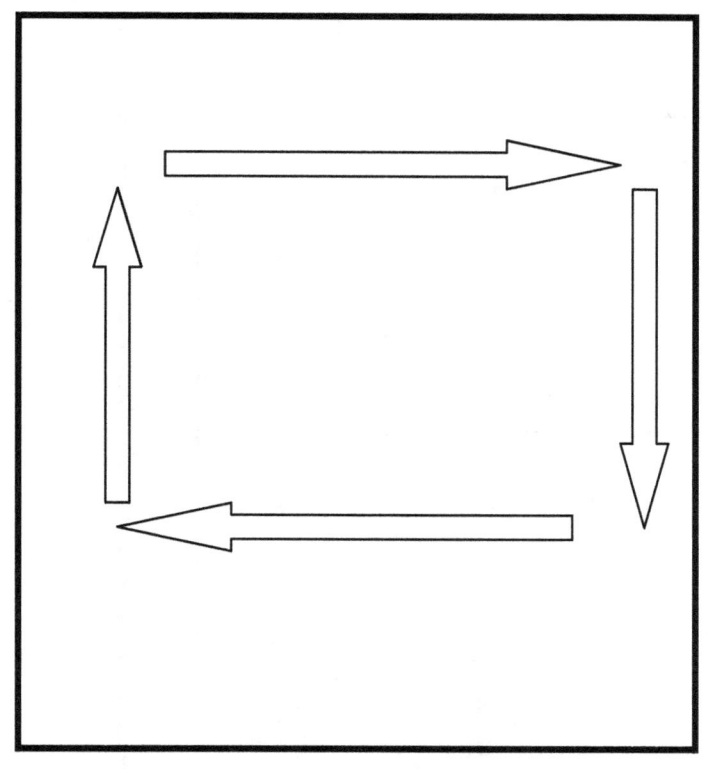
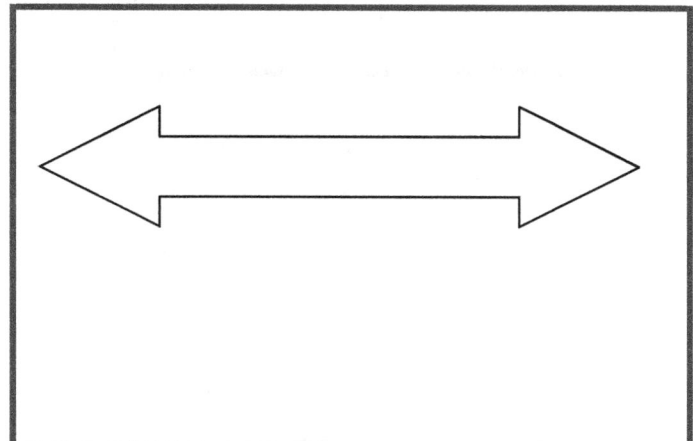

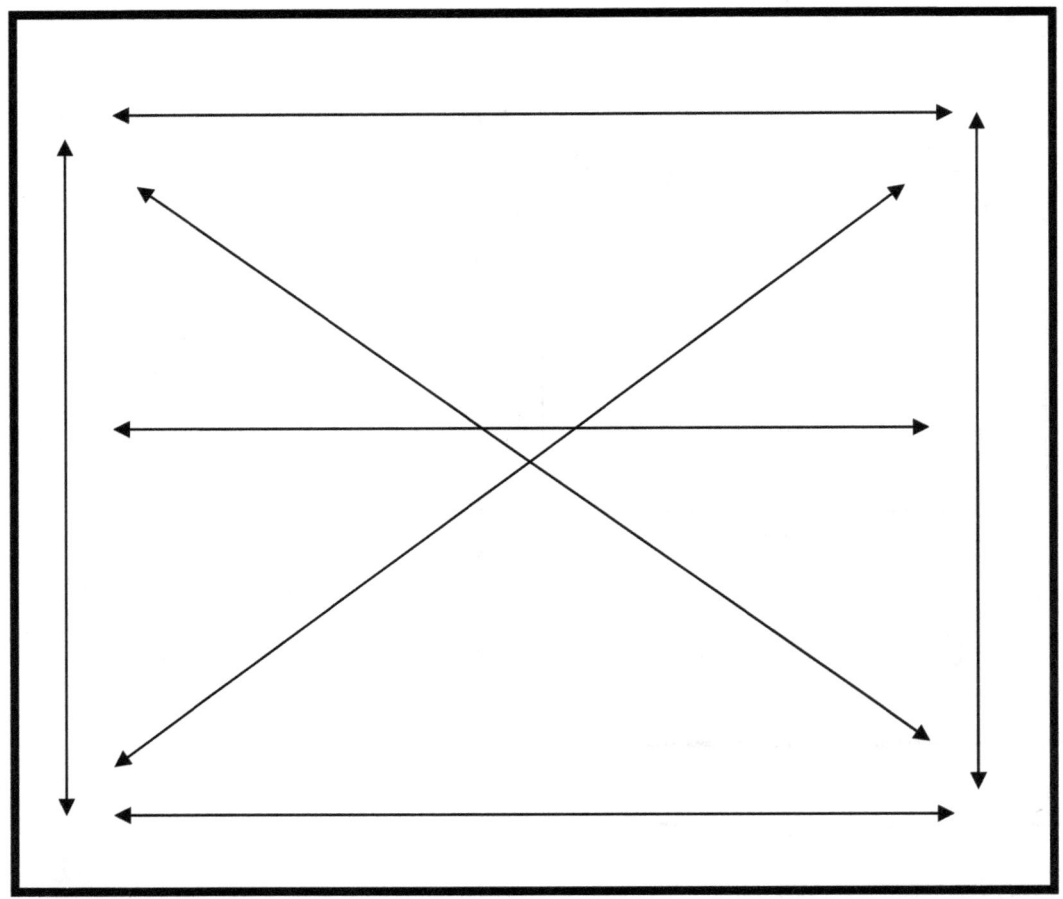

As you gaze at the arrows and allow your eyes to follow the direction, you can do so in straight lines or angles, or you can go in figure 8's or in other combinations of directions. The movement does not have to be rapid or at an uncomfortable pace. Notice any change or variation in the associations. This is only one way among many ways of altering or editing the associations, references, meanings, or sensory data configured within the sensory perceptive holographic mapping system.

End with systemic integration

Movement of energy in the body/mind

Energy in the body moves in some direction, and with some intensity. Notice where it starts, how it moves, does it seem frozen? Fast or slow moving? Does it have temperature? Is there some density? Does it have a texture? Where is it located in the body/mind?

Be curious, can you speed it up? Can you slow it down?

Notice if you can change the direction that the energy is moving. Reverse it.

Does the energy have a color? What is the color?

Change the color.

Does the energy have a label (emotion/feeling)?

Take the label off and have it as energy. Now let the energy do, what the energy does.

Notice the space that the energy is floating in. If the energy and the space are made of the same substance, notice what occurs. Now turn your attention around. What if anything did all of that?

Energy may be experienced like fiery ball, or it could feel like a block of ice. The energy could be described like a heavy bolder or a stone. Energy can be heavy or it could be light. Sometimes it could be described as numb, or absent like something is missing. The energy could be experienced as strong or weak, or like the energy is draining away. Be open to any way it is described and then expand the description.

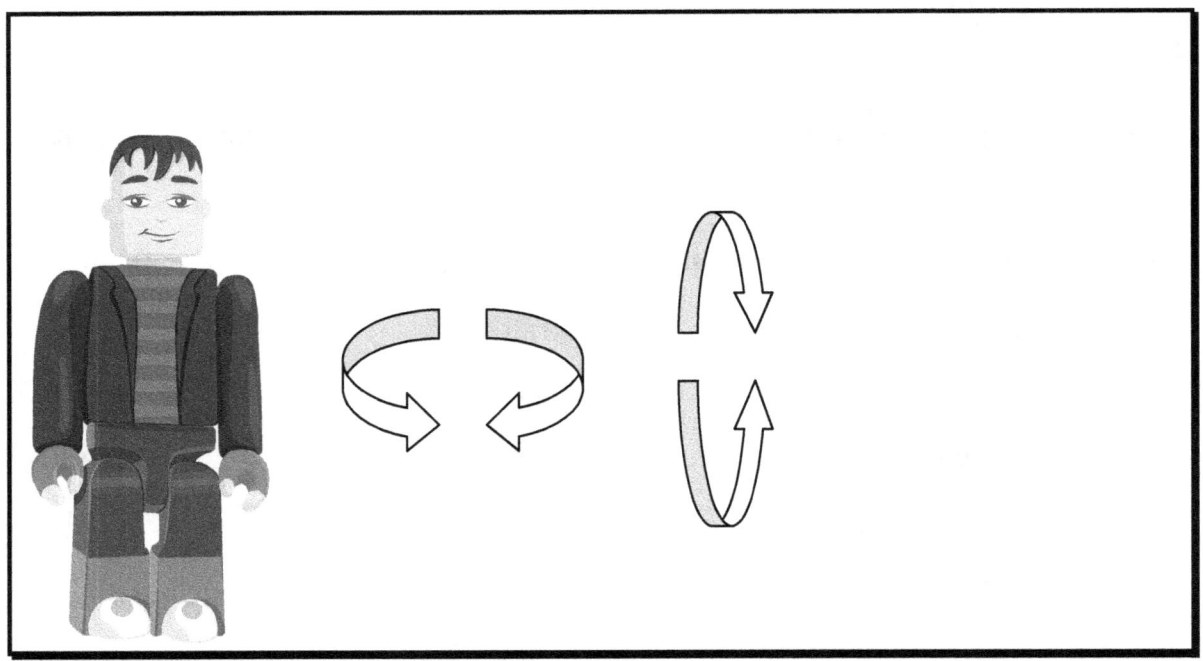

This comes from the work of Richard Bandler neuro-hypnotic re-patterning.

Past Experience — Present Time Position — Future Position

Context

Moment in time

Stimulus X

Cognition: Internal Processes
1. Visual Internal
.2. Auditory Internal

Feelings Emotions Internal State

Kinesthetic

Surface Skin

External Behavior + Representational Language

BMIR: Behavioral Manifestation of Internal Responses

When we begin to work on a problem it is just a slice of time. The person describes something that has occurred or is occurring and how it is a problem or challenge for them. They will then describe how thy want things to be or go in the future. We cannot see the images or scenes in their head, but the can describe them to us in exact detail. This is also true for what they are saying to themselves or the sounds they are hearing. We can observe changes in breathing, muscle tension, posture, eye movement, gestures and other changes in physiology. They can describe for us what they are experiencing internally with their feelings. Therefore, by asking question and eliciting their descriptions and how they internally represent their world we get a very exact map of the person challenge and often the solution or at least a reasonable alteration. *(Adapted from a workshop w/Ron Klein on EMI.) 2007*

Appendix

15 Styles of Distorted Thinking
Summary:

1. *Filtering:* You take the negative details and magnify them while filtering out all positive aspects of a situation.

2. *Polarized Thinking:* Things are black or white, good or bad. You have to be perfect or you're a failure. no middle ground

3. *Overgeneralization:* You come to a general conclusion based on a single incident or piece of evidence. If something bad happens once you expect it to happen over and over again.

4. *Mind Reading:* Without their saying so, you know what people are feeling and why they act the way they do. In particular, you are able to divine how people are feeling toward you.

5. *Catastrophizing:* You expect disaster . You notice o hear about a problem and start "what if's:" What if a tragedy strikes? What if it happens to you"

6. *Personalization:* Thinking that everything that people do or say is some kind of reaction to you. You also compare yourself to others, trying to determine who's smarter, better looking, etc.

7. *Control fallacy:* If you feel externally controlled, you see yourself as helpless, a victim of fate. The fallacy of internal control has you responsible or the pain and happiness of everyone around you.

8. *Fallacy of Fairness:* You feel resentful because you think you know what's fair but other people won't agree with you.

9. *Blaming:* You hold other people responsible for your pain, or take the other tact and blame yourself for every problem or reversal.

10. _Shoulds:_ You have a list of ironclad rules about how you and other people should act. People who break the rules anger you and you feel guilty if you violate the rules.
11. _Emotional Reasoning:_ You believe that what you feel must be true- automatically. If you _feel_ stupid and boring, then you must be stupid and boring.
12. _Fallacy of Change:_ You believe that other people will change to suit you if you just pressure or cajole them enough. You need to change people because your hopes for happiness seem to depend entirely on them.
13. _Global labeling:_ You generalize one or two qualities into a negative global judgment.
14. _Being right:_ you are continually on trail to prove that your opinions and actions are correct. Being wrong is unthinkable n you will go to any length to demonstrate your rightness.
15. _Heaven's Reward fallacy:_ you expect all your sacrifice and self-denial to pay off, as if there were someone keeping score. You feel bitter, when the reward doesn't come.

Chevreul's Pendulum

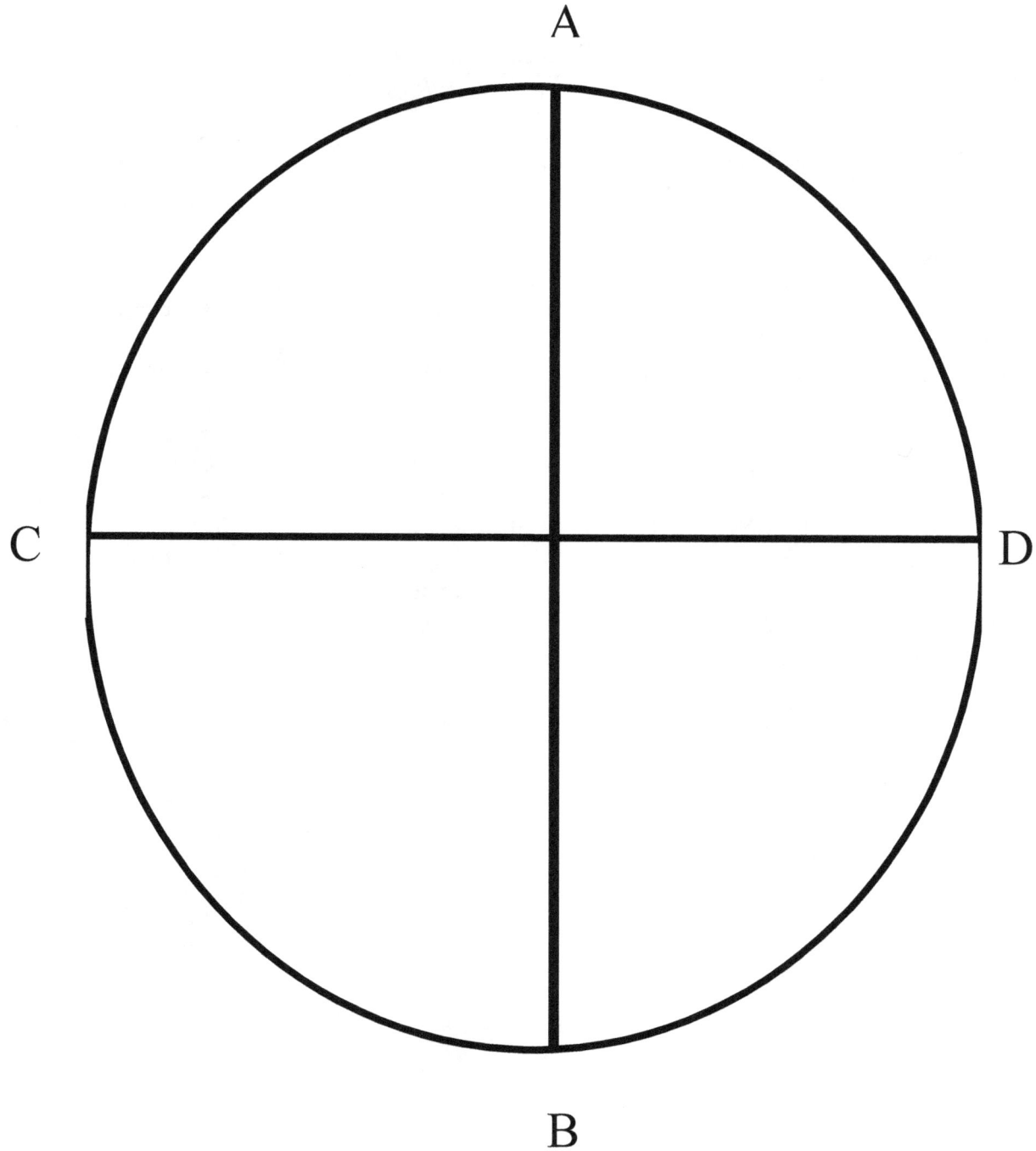

Facts * Stories * Experiences * Distinction
Bill O'Hanlon, MS

Facts	Stories	Experiences

❖ *Sensory Based Descriptions*	➢ Mind-reading
	· Thought & Feelings
	· Intentions & Purposes
	➢ Causes and Reasons
	➢ Predictions
	➢ Labeling Characterization
	➢ Generalizations
	➢ X-Y equivalences
	➢ Evaluations
	  .right & wrong
	  ..Good & Bad
		▪ Feelings
		▪ Sensations
		▪ Fantasies
		▪ Automatic thoughts

❖ *X=X* *No meanings added*		
❖ *Including the opposite possibility of meaning (or not)*		

Eclectic Therapy Press WWW.ECLECTICTHERAPIST.COM

FAMILY DEVELOPMENT AND DYNAMICS

THERE ARE THREE (3) DIMENSIONS TO EXPLORE AND THEY ARE ADAPTABILITY, COHESION AND COMMUNICATION.

ADAPTABILITY DIMENSION   RIGID - STRUCTURED - FLEXIBLE - CHAOTIC

LEADERSHIP	AUTHORITARIAN	WEAK
DISCIPLINE	STRICT	PERMISSIVE
NEGOTIATION	LIMITED	ENDLESS
ORGANIZED	OVER-ORGANIZED	DISORGANIZED
VALUES	INFLEXIBLE	SHIFTING

COHESION DIMENSION   DISENGAGED - SEPARATED - CONNECTED - ENMESHED

CLOSENESS	NOT CLOSE	TOO CLOSE
SUPPORT	NONE	TOO MUCH
DECISION MAKING	ONLY INDIVIDUAL	ONLY FAMILY
COMMONALITY	LITTLE	EVERYTHING
UNITY	NONE	TOTAL

INDIVIDUAL IDENTITY CYCLE

DEPENDENT   COUNTER-DEPENDENT   INDEPENDENT   INTERDEPENDENT

MARITAL/FAMILY COMMUNICATION STYLE:

	LOW ...> FACILITATING ...>	HIGH
1. LISTENER SKILLS		
A. *EMPATHY*	SELDOM	OFTEN
B. *ATTENTIVE LISTENING*		
2. SPEAKER SKILLS		
A. *FOR SELF*	SELDOM	OFTEN
B *FOR OTHERS*	OFTEN	SELDOM
3. SELF-DISCLOSURE	INFREQUENT	OFTEN
4. CLARITY	INCONSISTENT/UNCLEAR	CLEAR
5. CONTINUITY/TRACKING	INCONGRUENT	CONGRUENT
6. RESPECT AND REGARD	DISRESPECTFUL	RESPECTFUL

𝓔clectic 𝓣herapy 𝓟ress
www.eclectictherapist.com

Indirect Forms of Suggestion

1. **I***ndirect Associative Focusing*: [Raise a relevant topic without directing it in any manner at the manner.]

2. ***Truisms***: [Simple statement of fact about behavior that the client can readily accept.

You already know how to experience pleasant sensations like the **warmth** of the sun on your skin.
Everyone has had the experience of **nodding their head** yes or shaking it no even without quite realizing it.
We know when you sleep your unconscious can **dream**.
You can easily **forget** that dream when you awaken.
Sooner or later your hand is going to lift (eyes close, etc.)
Your headache [or whatever] will disappear **as soon as** your system is ready for it to leave.

3. Questions that Focus, Suggest, and Reinforce

Would you like to find a spot you can look at comfortably? As you continue looking at that spot, do your eyes get tired and have a tendency to blink? (pause) Will they close all at once or flutter a bit first as some parts of your body begin to experience the comfort so characteristic of trance? (pause) Does that comfort deepen as those eyes remain closed so you would rather not even try to open them? (pause) And how soon will you forget about your eyes and begin nodding your head very slowly as you dream a pleasant dream?

4. Implication

Now if you (sense the texture of your slacks on four (fingertips) {easy behavior}, it will probably remind you of (other experiences, of other feelings you have had.) {more relevant hypnotic behavior.}
If you sit down, you can go into trance.

ETP

The very complexity of mental functioning,//you go into trance to find out//a whole lot of things you can do,//and they are so may more than you dreamed of . (pause)

5. **Therapeutic Binds and Double Binds:** [when you give a client two or more alternatives, each leading to the same desired outcome.}

    Would you like to experience a light, medium, or deep trance?
    Would you like to go into a trance now or in a few minutes?

You don't have to listen to me because your unconscious is here and can hear what it needs to, respond in just the right way.

And it really doesn't matter what your conscious mind does because your unconscious automatically will do just what it needs to in order to achieve that anesthesia [age regression, catalepsy ,etc.]

As you continue resting in trance, does that pain {or whatever symptom} grow stronger or does it to fade in and out? Does it slowly change its location? Tell me whatever changes you notice in that pain [or whatever] in the next few minutes.

Let you head begin to nod very, very slowly when a feeling of warmth or coolness, prickliness, numbness, or whatever begins to develop in that pain area.

6. **Compound Suggestions:** {series of truisms to establish "yes set" or acceptance set so that suggestions will be readily accepted.

    Just look at one spot, and I am going to talk to you.

    Secret feeling you have never told anyone about//can be reviewed calmly within the privacy of your own mind//for help with current problems.

7. **Contingent Suggestions and Associational Networks:** {client's natural flow of voluntary responses is made contingent on the execution of hypnotic suggestion.}

"While you [any form of on-going or inevitable future Behavior], you can [Suggestion]."

"Don't [suggestion] until you [Behavior].

"The closer you get to [Behavior] the more you [Suggestion].

Your eyes will get tired and close all by themselves as you continue looking at that spot.

You will find yourself becoming more relaxed and comfortable as you continue sitting there with your eyes closed.

As you feel that deepening comfort you recognize you don't have to move, talk, or let anything bother you.

As the rest of your boy maintains that immobility so characteristic of a good hypnotic subject, your right hand will move the pencil across the page writing automatically something you would like to experience in trance.

8. **The Implied Directive:** {(1) a time binding introduction, (2) the implied or assumed suggestion and (3) behavioral response to signal when the implied suggestion has been accomplished.}

As soon as your unconscious knows//only you and my voice are here [or any suggested behavior] //your right hand will descend to your thigh.

As soon as your unconscious knows//it can again return to this state comfortably, and easily do constructive work the next time we are together,//you will find yourself awakening feeling refreshed and alert.

9. Open Ended Suggestions:

Every person has abilities not known to the self, abilities that can be expressed in trance.

There are memories, thoughts, feelings, and sensations completely or partially forgotten by the conscious mind. Yet they are available to the unconscious and can be experienced within trance now or later whenever the unconscious is ready.

10. Covering All Possibilities of Response :

Shortly your right hand, or I may be your left hand, will begin to lift up, or it may press down, or it may not move at all, but we will want to see just what happens. Maybe the thumb will be the fist, or you may feel something happening in your little finger, but the really important thing is not whether your hand lifts up or presses down or just remains still; rather, it is your ability to sense fully whatever feelings may develop in your hand.

11. Apposition of Opposites: {lightness & heaviness, warmth & coolness, relaxation & tension}.

You can **forget** to **remember** or **remember** to **forget**.

As your hand feels **light and lifts**, your eyelids will feel **heavy and close**.

12. Dissociation and Cognitive Overloading:

I want you to see someone sitting over there, and while working on that you can wonder what your hands are going to do. Will they lift up or down? Lifting the left had means no, and the right hand means yes, you will be able to see that visual image over there.

You can stand up or sit down. You can sit in that chair or the other. You can get out this door or that. You can come back to see me or refuse to see me. You can get well or remain sick. You can improve or you can get worse. You can accept therapy, or you can reject it. Or you can go into a trance to find out what you want.

You can as a person awaken, but you do not need to awaken as a body. (pause) You can awaken when your body awakens but without the recognition of your body.

Adapted from a training program, "Strategic Psychotherapy and Clinical Hypnosis" which was conducted by R. Reid Wilson in 1986. Also from The Collected Papers of Milton H. Erickson on Hypnosis Volume I. Irvington, 1980 Erickson and Rossi.

Eclectic Therapy Press.www.eclectictherapist.com

Levels of Consciousness

Level of Consciousness	Mental and Physical Characteristics	Example of Activity
Alert	1. Normal intellectual functioning 2. Normal reflexive and motor response.	You are playing tennis
Daydreaming *Light Trance*	1. Relaxation of body 2. Slowed breathing and pulse. 3. Withdrawal into self. 4. Direction of attention to imagined activity, dialogue, or event which may be possible or impossible.	You are idly thinking about playing tennis.
Moderate Trance	1. Loss of awareness of surroundings. 2. Closed eyes. 3. Increased awareness of internal functions, such as heartbeat or breathing. 4. Increased receptivity of senses. 5. Intensified imagery. 6. Literal interpretation of speech . (If asked, "Would you lift your arm? You would respond, "Yes.")	You are imaging yourself on a tennis court playing a game of tennis.
Deep Trance *Somnambulistic*	1. Further reduction of activity and energy output. 2. Limpness or stiffness of limbs. 3. Narrowing of attention. 4. Increased suggestibility. 5. Illusions of senses possible. 6. Loss of auditory receptivity and environmental awareness. 7. Heightened function of creative process.	You physically feel yourself playing tennis.
Sleep	1. Suspension of voluntary exercise. 2. Severe reduction or absence of conscious thought.	You dream of participating in a tennis match.

Categories of Memory

Process	*Explicit*= Declarative Conscious	*Implicit*= Non-declarative Unconscious
Information Types	Cognitive Facts Mind Verbal/semantic Description of Operations Description of Procedures	Emotional Conditioning Body Sensory Automatic skills Automatic procedures
Mediating Limbic Structure	Hippocampus	Amygdala
Maturity	Around 3 years	From birth
Activity during Traumatic event and/or flashback	Suppressed	Activated
Language	Constructs narrative	Speechless

AUTONOMIC NERVOUS SYSTEM (SMOOTH MUSCLES, INVOLUNTARY)

Sympathetic Branch

Activates during positive and negative stress states, including sexual climax, rage, desperation, terror, anxiety/panic, trauma.

Noticeable Signs

Faster respiration
Quicker heart rate (pulse)
Increased blood pressure
Pupils dilate
Pale skin color
Increased sweating
Skin cold (possibly clammy)
Digestion (and peristalsis) decreases

During actual traumatic event OR with flashback (visual, auditory and/or sensory)

Preparation for quick movement, leading to possible fight reflex or flight reflex.

Parasympathetic Branch

States of activation include rest and relaxation, sexual arousal, happiness, anger, grief, sadness.

Noticeable Signs

Slower deeper respiration
Slower heart rate (pulse)
Decreased blood pressure
Pupils constrict
Flushed skin color
Skin dry (usually warm) to touch
Digestion (and peristalsis) increases

During actual traumatic event OR with flashback *(visual, auditory and/or sensory)*

Can also activate concurrently with, while masking, sympathetic activation leading to tonic immobility; freezing reflex (like a mouse, caught by a cat, going dead). Marked by simultaneous signs of high sympathetic and parasympathetic activation.

Organization of the Central Nervous System:

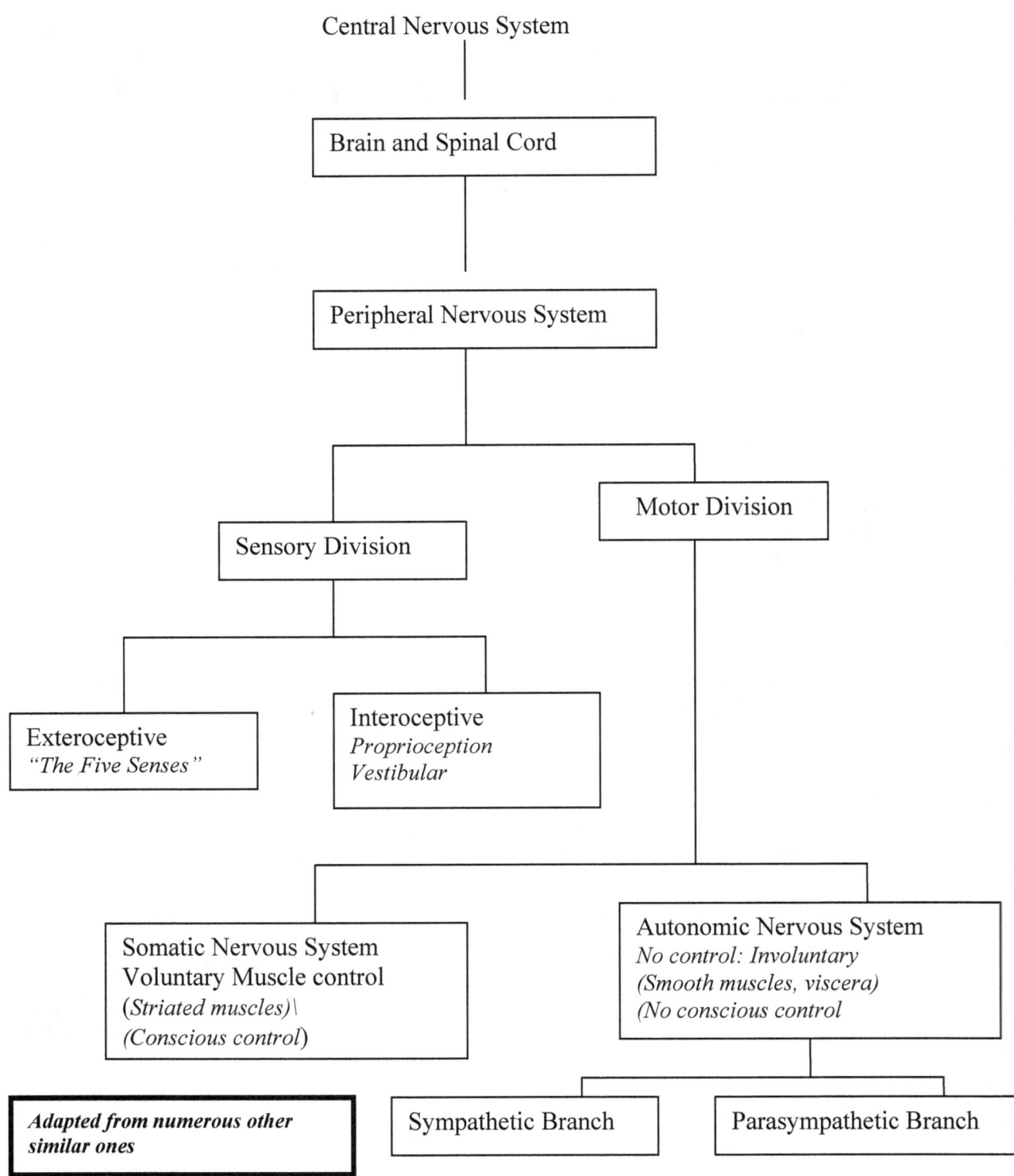

Post-Hypnotic Suggestions

I. **Post –Hypnotic Suggestions**: Any suggestion after the patient achieves trance to be carried out after the patient terminates trance. Anything you say during trance which is accepted becomes a post-hypnotic suggestion. The client can choose to use anything as a P-H suggestion.

   Used to provide clients with an opportunity to develop insight, experience the potential for change, integrate behavior.

II. **Post Hypnotic Cues**: Actions, thoughts, words, images, or events that initiate or trigger a suggested response. (Example: light switch off and yawn…..> sleepiness.)

III. **Therapist's Task**: to place p-h suggestion in a framework that allows client to use it in a practical way.

   Client will believe/experience behavior is self-ordered and spontaneous.

IV. **How:**

   1. *Link* suggestion to inevitable piece of behavior, such as things that naturally occur in day, week, or month. Use a time-binding introduction of implied behavior- *"When you come to the breakfast table."*
   2. *Accept* the client's descriptive words and turn them back on him in p-h suggestion--→ gives client a feeling of being committed to his own intentions/wishes and intensifies his ability to act accordingly without feeling forced.

3. P-H suggestion through questions. Would you like to have?... Rhetorical

4. The silver platter method: Direct suggestions which are desired by the client's conscious mind, one's which the client has stated or implied that he/she will readily accept. Absorb the message.

5. Feel free to over-detail exact instructions.

6. Repeatedly, emphatically, and insistently.

7. More you repeat them, the more effective they will be.

8. Disarm the client. Get him involved in thinking about something else, so meaningful suggestions can be accepted without conscious walls being up.

9. Use confusion. Offers conscious involvement in word games so the unconscious an accept suggestions/work.

10. Don't say "When you come out of trance you will find..."Say, "I wonder how...?" "When...?" "How much...?" " Do you suppose it would be possible for...?" "I'd be curious to know...?"

11. Implications: P-H suggestions that presuppose change. "Today in trance, this is simply a time to teach you comfort relaxation..." "How soon will you...?" "As soon as you..." "One of the many ways you can..." "After you have..."

12. Anecdote re: gradual, imperceptible changes or changes over time: rain barrel filling up; rain drenching the earth,

snowball rolling down hill, squeezing a tennis ball daily leading to strength (place in a metaphor: "I had a friend once who...")

13. Use initial phase of troubling behavior as a cue for surprising response or specific coping response (thought, feeling, action, dissociation). When.
    1. All the time.
    2. Use special hypnotic response/phenomena as opportunity to generalize p-h suggestion.
    3. When client experiences something new, surprising, ego-building---→ imply connection.
    4. When client is feeling positive, good about himself or current experience.
    5. People drop defenses when you say "In a minute I'm going to terminate this trance experience with you." Good time to intervene.
    6. Use direct suggestions as client is rising out of trance.

Amnesia Suggestions

Amnesia can be given directly, emphatically and repetitiously as specific instruction, rather than casual, incidental admonition or suggestion.

"An experience of forgetting in itself is an experience which is not alien t anybody"

"Nothing sufficiently important for conscious recollection has been said."

"Say, why don't you just forget what I've been talking about and place it in the back of your mind. Good place for it, can't forget it there."

"Take a nice leisurely walk home, thinking about nothing"

"Fade away like a dream…"

"Lock you memories in your unconscious."

Postulates for the Creed of Eclectic Therapist.

These postulates are interwoven into the eclectic therapist's mapping system, which is based on the best information available to the therapist now. As the Eclectic therapist is always attempting alignment with the territory and the mapping system of the client, the therapists' map remains open to updating. The therapist's map is subject to change as it is better informed by interaction with the territory and the client.

We find that for the most part that all forms of effective psychotherapy utilize the following principles. These are true except when they are not. The map represents the territory but is not the territory.

All effective therapy is biological, therefore changes in thinking, feeling, believing, expressing or behaving creates biological change and comes from biological change.

Effective therapy involves a connection between the one individual (therapist) and some inner resources within the other individual (client). Therapy is a biological interaction.

Effective therapy involves interruption/deconstruction of territorially incongruent sensory alteration states (trance) and the construction or alignment and replacement of territorially congruent sensory states.

Effective therapy involves the rearranging and updating of biologically encoded programming to bring about a change.

Effective therapy addresses two phases of intervention 1. Acceptance by the organism of the intervention and 2. Change of the encoded programming once the intervention has been accepted.

Effective therapy recognizes a homeostatic function/status quo tendency of the organism. Each of us is attempting to stay in balance with the flow of energy in the river of life. Mapping directs the navigation and homeostasis is the gyroscope.

Effective therapy is respectful to the homeostatic system of both the therapist and the client. Respect for the mapping system of each. Maps are not right are wrong they are attempts to assimilate sensory data (stimulation) within the individuals' ability to sense, interpret and integrate the flow within it's existing mapping system.

All therapies are maps to the territory of the client's world, but the effective therapists' map is recognized as a map and not the actual territory. Awareness allows us to recognize that maps are biological, abstract representations of the experiencing of life's movement.

Effective psychotherapy recognizes the organism's need for closure to reduce/eliminate vacuums in the client's knowledge of the world. The Completion /or Gestalt Closure Error is a naturally occurring attempt by the individual to locate itself within energy, mass and space-time. Within the internal holographic representation of the experiential world, the individual attempts to know, predict and control outcomes and survive. Different scenarios are created, offered and played out in the nervous system's efforts to survive.

Effective therapy recognizes that the organism is one unit. Further, there is recognition that the establishment of the concepts of mind and body are artificial contrivances not a representation of the true nature of the client or the client's experience. One substance is described and talked about as if it were infinite substances. There are no substances there are only abstract representations of substances and their imagined interactions.

Effective therapy recognizes the organism will resist change by filtering, modifying and otherwise distorting incoming sensory data that are not consistent with the basic preexisting programming of the organism developed during the ongoing socialization period. Biological variance is dealt with by attempts to stay balanced. The map is the biology's effort to represent its interaction and its changes within its appearance and disappearance.

According to Quantum physics being here and not here occurs approximately 14 times per second. The biology resists the void, which is itself. Words are the organism's effort to describe the indescribable.

Effective therapy generally follows a principle of requisite variety. Greater flexibility generally means more effective adaptation.

In effective therapists' map, the organism and its environment are one and represented in that way. . The various aspects of the client's sensory perceptive map include all aspects of the client's world including the known and unknown parts.

Effective therapy recognizes communication by the organism is biological and includes both verbal and nonverbal expressions from the organisms' map.

Eclectic Therapy Press. www.eclectictherapist.com

Sensory System Words

Mark each of the following lists of words as being primarily (V) visual, (A) Auditory (K) kinesthetic or (OG) olfactory/gustatory or (N) none.

A clear day _____

Churned up _____

Doing it now _____

Colorful idea _____

Tuning it _____

Insensitive _____

Looking back _____

Something is missing _____

Envision my needs _____

Pungent concept _____

Shaken up _____

Get hold of it _____

Follow my nose _____

Walk over you _____

Get a perspective _____

Out of rhythm _____

Nose to the grindstone _____

Resonates with me _____

Open yourself to me _____

Front line _____

Out of place _____

Grinding inside _____

Looking back _____

Clear as a bell _____

Stumbling block _____

Soft sell _____

A little hazy _____

Touch me _____

Trip me up _____

Run ragged _____

New idea _____

Sweet idea _____

Dim concept _____

Smell a rat _____

Speak to me of your sadness _____

Tone of voice _____

A salty speech _____

A good note _____

Walk through life _____

Images from the past _____

One step at a time _____

Yesterday's dinner _____

Eclectic Therapy Press.*www.eclectictherapist.com*

Sample Suggestions

Concentration:
1. Every day in every way, my concentration powers steadily increase.
2. I am completely absorbed and fully engrossed in whatever I am doing.
3. I find all of my subjects becoming more interesting.
4. I am concentrating better and better every day, especially when I study.

Retention:
1. Retention of everything I learn is lasting and permanent.
2. Day by day, my retention span is steadily increasing.

Recall:

1. Recalling information I need becomes easier every day.
2. Whatever I have learned I can easily and readily recall.
3. Recalling information I need comes so easily, It's as though I had just finished reading or hearing it.

Confidence:

1. I am more poised and confident in all of my daily situations.
2. Confidence in myself grows by leaps and bounds daily.
3. I am more highly motivated and confident in whatever I undertake.

Becoming Outgoing:

1. I am becoming more outgoing every day.
2. I am becoming interested in other people and in events outside of myself.
3. I am deriving pleasure and excitement from dealing with others.
4. Dealing with people and their problems is adding enthusiasm and zest to my life.

Sub-Modality Distinctions

Visual	**Some Questions to Elicit the Distinction**
Color/ black and white	Is it in color or black and white? Is it full color spectrum? Are the colors vivid or washed out?
Brightness	In that context, is it brighter or darker than normal?
Contrast	Is it high contrast (vivid) or washed out?
Focus	Is the image sharp in focus or is it fuzzy?
Texture	Is the image smooth or rough textured?
Detail	Are there foreground and back ground details? Do you see the details as part of the whole or do you have to shift focus to see them?
Size	How big is the picture? Ask for specific, estimated size, like 11" x 14"
Distance	How far away is the image? (again ask for specific, estimated distance like 6')
Shape	What shape is the picture: square, rectangular, round, oval, etc?
Border	Is there a border around it or do the edges fuzz out? Does the border have a color? How thick is the border?
Location	Where is the image located in space? Show me with both hands where you see the image(s).

Sub-Modality Distinctions

Visual	Some Questions to Elicit the Distinction
Movement: Within the image	Is it a movie or is it a still picture? How rapid is the movement: faster or slower than normal?
Of the image	Is the image stable? What direction does it move in? How fast is it moving?
Orientation	Is the picture tilted?
Associated/Dissociated	Do you see yourself or do you see the event as if you were there?
Perspective	From what perspective do you see it? (If dissociated) Do you see yourself from the right or left, back or front?
Proportion	Are the people and the things in the image in proportion to one another and to yourself or are some of them larger or smaller than life?
Dimension	Is it flat or is it three dimensional? Does the picture wrap around you?
Singular/Plural	Is there one image or more than one? Do you see them one after the other or at the same time?

Auditory

Location	Do you hear it from the inside or from the outside? Where does the sound (voice) originate?
Pitch	Is it high pitched or low pitched? Is the pitch higher or lower than normal?

Sub-Modality Distinctions

Auditory	**Some Questions to Elicit the Distinction**
Tonality	What is the tonality: nasal, full and rich, thin, grating?
Melody	Is it monotone or is there a melodic range?
Inflection	Which parts are accentuated?
Volume	How loud is it?
Tempo	Is it fast or slow?
Rhythm	Does it have a beat or a cadence?
Duration	Is it continuous or intermittent?
Mono/Stereo	Do you hear it on one side, both sides, or is the sound all around you?

Kinesthetic	
Quality	How would you describe the body sensation: tingling, warm, cold, relaxed, tense, knotted, diffused?
Intensity	How strong is the sensation?
Location	Where do you feel it in your?
Movement	Is there movement in the sensation? Is the movement continuous or does it come in waves?
Direction	Where does the sensation start? How does it get from the place of origin to the place where you are most aware of it?
Speed	Is it a slow steady progression or does it move in a rush?
Duration	Is it continuous or intermittent?

Six-Step Reframing

1. Identify the pattern (X) to be changed. "I want to stop X' ing, but I can't." or "I want to Y, but something stops me."

2. Establish communication with the part responsible for the pattern.
    a) "Will the part of me that makes me X communicate with me in consciousness?" Pay attention to any feelings, images, or sounds that occur in response to asking that question internally.

    b) Establish "yes/no" meaning with the signal. Have it increase in brightness, volume or intensity for "yes" and decrease for "no".

3. Separate the behavior; pattern X, from the positive intention of the part that is responsible for X. The unwanted behavior is only a way to achieve some positive function.
    a) Ask the part that runs X "Would you be willing to let me know in consciousness what you are trying to do for me with pattern X?"

    b) If you get a "yes" response, ask the part to go ahead and communicate its intention. If you get a "no" response, proceed with unconscious reframing, presupposing positive intention.

    c) Is that intention acceptable to consciousness? Do you want to have a part of you that fulfills that function?

    d) Ask that part that runs X "If there were ways to accomplish your positive function that would work as well or better than X, would you be interested in trying them out?"

4. Access a creative part, and generate new behaviors to accomplish the positive function.

    a) Access experiences of creativity and anchor them, or ask "Are you aware of a creative part of yourself?"

    b) Have that part runs X communicate its positive function to the creative part, allow the creative part to generate more choices to accomplish that function, and have the part that used to run

Six-Step Reframing- continued

X select 3 choices that are at least as good as or better than X. Have it give a "yes" signal each time it selects such an alternative.

5. Ask the part "Are you willing to take responsibility for using the three new alternatives in the appropriate context?" This provides future- pace. You can additionally ask the part at the unconscious level to identify the sensory cues that will trigger the new choices, and to experience fully what it's like to have those sensory cues effortlessly and automatically bring on one of the new choices.

6. Ecological check. "Is there any part of me that objects to any of the three new alternatives?" If there is a "yes" response, recycle to step # 2 above.

Tell the part, "Thank-you" each time it communicates.

THE STRUCTURAL DEVELOPMENT CONTINUUM

HIGH

Affective

Affective stability
High anxiety tolerance
Anxiety serves as a signal

Good self-soothing abilities
Good differentiation of feelings
Smooth modulation of feelings
High frustration tolerance
Experience of cohesion
Insusceptible to regressive states

Cognitive

Objective self-perception (good "observing ego")
Constancy of self-perception
Predominance of mature defenses
Mature development of moral sense
High-quality reality perception
High quality of judgment
High quality of synthetic abilities
Formulation and execution of clear intentions
Regressions creative and ego mediated
Projections or regressions "owned"

Interpersonal

Object constancy
Good self-other differentiation
Distance and closeness well modulated

Intimate others usually assumed to show object constancy

Perception of others reality based

LOW

Affective

Affect highly labile
Low anxiety tolerance
Anxiety traumatic and disorganizing

Poor self-soothing abilities
Poor differentiation of feelings
Feelings under modulated
Low frustration tolerance
Self-fragmentation
Susceptible to regressive states

Cognitive

Self-perception not reality based

Self-splitting
Predominance of immature defenses
Morality founded on immature basis

Poor reality perception
Impaired judgment
Impaired synthetic abilities
Intentions and planning impaired

Regressions not ego mediated

Projections and regressions not "owned"

Interpersonal

Object splitting
Blurring of boundaries
Relationships characterized by clinging, detachment, or ambivalence
Relationships characterized by fears of other's abandonment, rejection, or destructiveness.
Relationship characterized by merger, twinship, mirroring, idealization.

Eclectic Therapy Press.www.

Therapeutic Use of Trance Phenomena

Dissociation	- view anxiety-provoking/traumatic scene without discomfort - rehearse new learning - prepare for other trance phenomena - separate from pain
Age Regression	- relive a trauma - retrieve a needed resource - go back to a time before the symptom or belief - investigate facts of a past event
Hypermnesia	- gather diagnostic information - clarify details of a past event - Speech/test/event preparation
Time Distortion	- decrease length of pain, anxiety or other symptom - increase comfortable time - prepare for Age Regression or Pseudo-Orientation - prolong sexual function - increase time between hunger
Pseudo-Orientation In Time	- thinking, feeling, believing differently in face of old memory - change portions of problematic imagery - go to the future and experience success - plan "backward" from success - change personal history
Positive Hallucination	- intensify a resource - rehearse new learning - create supportive figure/object
Negative Hallucination	- not notice uncomfortable stimuli (crowds, feared objects, etc. - not notice symptoms/pain
Amnesia	- protect from trauma - post-hypnotic suggestions - forget past symptom/pain - forget pain sensations in the future
Analgesia/Anesthesia	- protect incomplete therapeutic work until next session - Pain management

Visual- Auditory- Kinesthetic Words

Visual	Auditory	Kinesthetic
Watched	Asked	Burdened
Envision	Complain	Hurt
Gape	Mumble	Muffled
Sighted	Silenced	Run
Expose	Chatter	Sweep
Gleam	Weep	Flop
Surface	Mention	Tremble
Attractive	Noisy	Plush
Glow	Echo	Scrambled
Detected	Questioned	Slipped
Inspected	Stammered	Pressured
Foresee	Disagree	Crumbled
Grin	Cry	Bounce
Staring	Humming	Brushing
Obscure	Vocal	Mushy
Clear	Request	Share
Dark	Silent	Comfy
Spy	Utter	Pitch
Appear	Argue	Break
Preview	Shriek	Trample
Cloudy	Melodic	Smooth
Bright	Shouting	Shaky
Sparkling	Gurgling	Hugging
Peering	Recite	Crouching
Observe	Sang	Pull
Glowed	Lecture	Skipped
Reflect	Tell	Collect
Blindly	Shrill	Grind
Eyed	Expressed	Held
Displayed	Translate	Stuffed
Grin	Sighs	Weigh
Reflects	Called	Fits
Concealed	Grumble	Slipped
Search	Quiet	Wash
Shiny	Discuss	Soft
View	Tell	Hold
Reveal	Inquire	Beat
Gaze	Loud	Touch
Blurred	Insult	Warm
Veil	Growl	Litter
Sightsee	Announce	Pinch
Admire	Repeat	Build

Visual- Auditory- Kinesthetic Words-continued

Visual	Auditory	Kinesthetic
Glance	Sounds	Bends
Scan	Yell	Feel
Show	Reply	Grab
Perceive	Talk	Force
Exhibit	Cheer	Twist
Disappear	Resonant	Work
Graphic	Answer	Grasp
Vanish	Hear	Grapple
Focus	Chat	Suffered
See	Enumerate	Feel
Fantasize	Explained	Carry
Faced	Listen	Thick

V-K Dissociation

The steps for utilizing three-place visual-kinesthetic dissociations are:

1. Establish a powerful anchor for solid comfort.
2. Holding the anchor, have the client visualize himself out in front in the very first scene of the traumatic/problematic incident, making it a "still-shot." So he is sitting there, next to you, seeing his younger self before him.
3. When he can see himself clearly, have him float out of his body so that so he can see himself sitting there next to you watching his younger self. As such, there are now three of him. The visual perspective remains from the third place. Their actual body is in the second place and the younger self going through the experience is in the first place. When this three place dissociation is accomplished anchor it.
4. Now have the person run the experience through, making sure he remains kinesthetically dissociated from the incident by the use of anchors and by the use of verbal patterns which separate out of the three places—*him, there, the younger you, that experience, what happened then*, to separate the younger traumatized self from—*you, here, today, watching yourself,* etc.
5. When the experience has been completely seen, have the third place float back into the second place. (So the visual perspective is being integrated with the actual body position of the client).

6. Have the present-day person go to the younger one (the one who went through the experience) and have reassure him that he is from the future; giving the younger self needed comfort and appreciation.
7. When the present-day person can see that the visualized younger self understands, have him integrate by bringing that younger part back inside his own body.

The following diagram will serve to illustrate and clarify the steps:
You anchor the client (2) to feel secure in the here and now, then the client visualizes his younger self [1], he floats out of his body to the visual perspective of (3). Anchor this disassociative state from 3 the incident is run thru. After which 3 integrates back to 2. Then 2 comforts and reassures 1 and finally 2 brings 1 back into 2 and only you and your client are there.

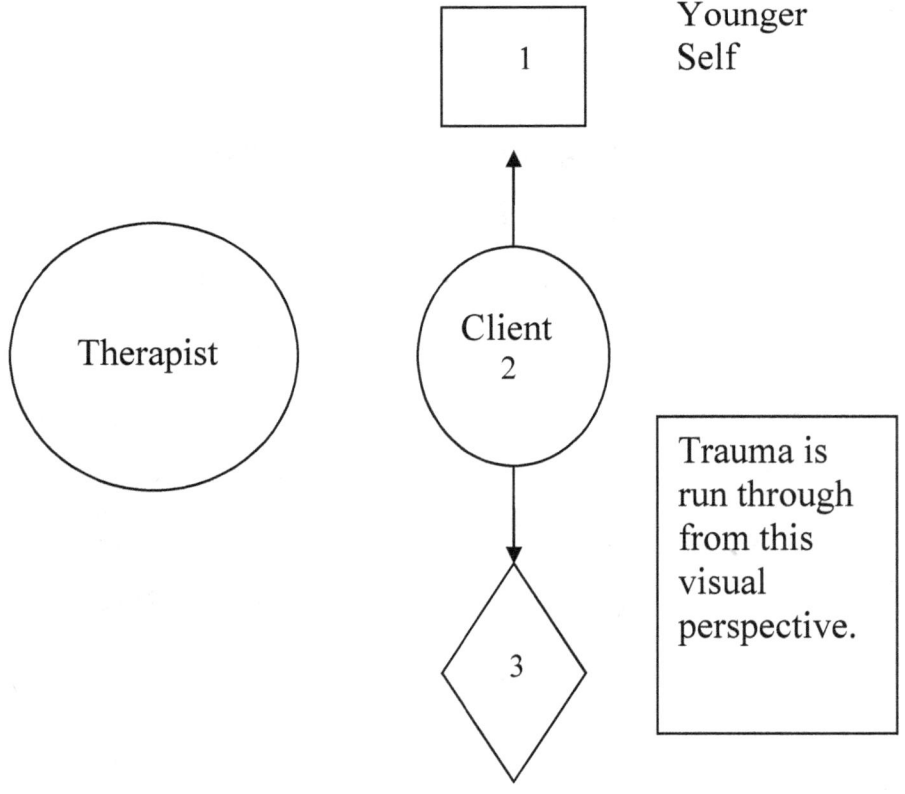

Playing Squash & Swisher Sweets

Exercise: Visual Squash:

1. Create a vivid representation of yourself the way you are now (present state), with all your difficulties.

2. See yourself the way you would be if you got through all the problems. Be very clear on how you will be behaving, what you will be saying and feeling. Make the image as clear and rich in detail as possible, Use all of your senses.

3. Place one image in each hand of your hands outstretched in front of you with a space separating them. This space represents the unexplored territory and unspecified steps that lie between the two states.

4. Begin to make a series of images or movies of the logical steps from one state to the other. Adjust each picture or movie, frame by frame, changing whatever needs to be changed, until each is fully representational, progressive stage of the process of change.

5. When you have between ten and twelve stages in front of you, begin slowly to close your hands, collapsing all the stages into a single process.

6. Bring your clasped hands toward your body, making a new feeling that represents action and success.

7. Spin that feeling faster and faster, intensifying it to spread throughout your body, so it permeates every muscle, every organ, every nerve, and every cell. As you do this, look at where you want to go and decide clearly what you need to do first. Then see yourself taking the second step, then the third step, and keep spinning and intensifying the feeling until you feel compelled to get up and go for it.

Exercise Swish Pattern:

1. Think of a feeling, response, or behavior that you would like to change. This format is particularly useful in dealing with feelings that seem to compel people to act in ways that do not match their self-image.

2. Close your eyes and see what happens from an associated point of view. If it is a behavior, identify the trigger point of the sequence. Put a border around it and make it bright and intense.

3. Now see yourself (dissociated) as if you have already made the change. See how you will be acting; hear what you will be hearing. Be sure that this representation is preferable to the one in Step 2.

4. Shrink the image of your desired state down to a small, dark square and place it in the corner of the first image that you made.

5. Now, darken and shrink the large image down as you simultaneously brighten and enlarge the second image until it completely covers the first one. Hear or make the sound s-w-i-s-h as you do so. Open your eyes to break state.

Exercises from Richard Bandler's *Guide to Trance-formation.* 2008, Deerfield Beach, Florida. Health Communications, Inc.

KEY TERMS

1. Cognitive Programming:

Any information housed in the *neural information centers* and thus part of the *sensory perceptive holographic mapping, system*. This information can be accurate or inaccurate.

2. Cognitive Programming Errors:

Misinformation encoded into the *neural information centers* of the organism that is incongruent with the reality of the environment of the organism. This misinformation, consequently, leads to dysfunctional *SPA* (*trance*) states.

3. Congruent Cognitive Programming:

Programming that leads to congruent *SPA* states and therefore facilitates congruent interaction between the organism and the environment.

4. Descartes' Error:

Descartes' Error is dividing the mind/body into various parts as if it were separated into mind and body. This further leads to a division of thought and feelings, which then leads to the argument and debate over primacy, origination, and causation.

5. Dissonance:

Dissonance is the state created when the accepted pool of programming stored in the biology is threatened by incoming information or shifts in information and thereby threatens a disturbance of the biology of the organism. Cognitive *dissonance* as it has been defined is a smaller subset of this larger action.

6. Eclectic:

Being *eclectic* means to gather from or, to select from various doctrines or methods, choosing what appears to be the best from among the various doctrines, methods, or styles. *Eclectic* is composed of elements drawn from various sources, also heterogeneous (*Merriam-Webster Online Dictionary*).

7. Gestalt Closure Errors:

The tendency of the mapping system of the organism to seek closure where there is a deficit, incomplete stimulus, or information available to make a decision or render a judgment is called *Gestalt closure*. This creates confabulatory errors, which are the merging of actual sensory stimuli with internally generated material.

8. Homeostasis:

Homeostasis is a description of the ongoing mechanism that attempts to maintain sameness within the biological system. It does not involve a decision of right or wrong; good or bad, but simply is about maintaining the status quo. Thought as a biological process is part of the biological system.

9. Neural Information Center:

This component is part programming, part electro-chemical, and involves both afferent and efferent pathways. In other words, this unit is a hybrid of the *neural information centers* mapping and biology that sends instruction and directs programming into the physiology of the organism, as well as receives feedback from the physiological responses of the organism and movement back into the center. The information within a particular *neural information center* and cluster of *neural information centers* is responsible for directing the various *SPA trance* experiences. It is therefore understood that these are the basic building blocks of the *sensory perceptive mapping system* of the organism.

10. Persistent Patterns of Trance Clusters:

Persistent patterns which create the illusion of identity formed by the overlapping of *sensory perceptive alteration* states that are present and largely predictable, in a particular organism. These patterns are idiosyncratic in nature. These apparently predictable patterns are relatively stable but are impacted by variations in stimuli coming from within the biological organism and from the external environment.

11. Semantic Reversal Mechanism:

This mechanism is part of the *homeostatic* system designed to protect the map. Its function is to neutralize incoming information that threatens *dissonance* to the organism. *Semantic reversal mechanisms* involve semantic alterations of the incoming stimuli, such as the addition of "not," inclusion of "yes, but" formulations, and pseudo-logical argumentations. Further, neutralization effects can be visual with images that attempt to counter the incoming threatening information.

12. Sensory Perceptive Holographic Mapping:

Mapping is a multi-sensorial, multi-dimensional, interactive, navigational system, which directs the organism's interactions with the environment both internally and externally. Contained within this mapping system is the flight/fight/freeze mechanism, as well as a completion mechanism. The mapping is balanced by *homeostasis*.

13. Socialization:

Socialization is an ongoing, interactive mapping process whereby the individual continues to adjust his programming in response to the programming of those in his environment. This obviously can influence pre-existing programming. As Alfred Korzybski reminds us, "The Map is not the territory." *Socialization* can lead to congruent or highly incongruent programming.

14. Trance:

Sensory perceptive alteration "SPA" is an integral function of *homeostasis* and dictated by the *sensory perceptive mapping* and the *neural information centers* that construct that map. *SPA* is a state (or series of states) that edits the sensory stimulus to be consistent with the *neural information center* programming already existing.

15. Trauma:

The state which occurs when information or stimuli entering the organism is not assimilated, accommodated, or synthesized into the *sensory mapping system*, thereby causing a response from the *homeostatic* defense mechanism. Attempts to contain the unassimilated, neural information can result in Post-traumatic Stress Disorder symptoms, such as flashbacks, intrusive memories, and emotional fluctuations.

Bibliography

Almaas, A. H. (1986). The Void. Berkeley, California: Diamond Books.

----------------(1996). The Point of Existence. Berkeley, California: Diamond Books.

----------------(1998). Essence With The Elixir of Enlightenment. York Beach, Maine: Samuel Weiser, Inc.

----------------(1987). Diamond Heart Book One: The Real Man. Berkeley, California: Diamond Books.

----------------(1987). Diamond Heart Book Two: The Freedom To Be. Berkeley, California: Diamond Books.

----------------(1990). Diamond Heart Book Three: Being And The Meaning Of Life. Berkeley, California: Diamond Books.

----------------. (1992). Work on the Super Ego. Berkeley, California: Diamond Books.

----------------. (1998). Facets Of Unity: The Enneagram Of Holy Ideas. Berkeley, California: Diamond Books.

----------------(1998). The Pearl Beyond Price. Berkeley, California: Diamond Books. American Psychiatric Association (1994). Diagnostic and Statistical Manuel of Mental Disorders–TR, (4th Edition). Washington, D.C.: Author.

Andreas, Connirae; Andreas Steve (1987). Change Your Mind and Keep the Change. Moab, Utah: Real People Press.

----------------(1989). Heart of the Mind. Moab, Utah: Real People Press.

Andreas, Steve (2006) Six Blind Elephants Understanding Ourselves and Each Other, Volume I: Fundamental Principles of Scope and Category. Moab Utah: Real People Press.

----------------(2006). Six Blind Elephants Understanding Ourselves and Each Other, Volume II. Applications and Explorations of Scope and Category. Moab, Ut: Real People Press

Bandler, Richard (2008). Guide to Trance-Formation. Deerfield Beach, Florida Health Communications, Inc.

Bandler, Richard (2008). Get The Life You Want. Deerfield Beach, Florida. Health Communications, Inc.

Bandler, Richard & Grinder, John (1975). Patterns of the Hypnotic Techniques of Milton H. Erickson, MD, Volume I. Scotts Valley, California: Meta Publications.

----------------(1975). Patterns of the Hypnotic Techniques of Milton H. Erickson, MD, Volume II. Scotts Valley, California: Meta Publications.

----------------(1975). The Structure of Magic, Volume I. Palo Alto, California: Science and Behavior Books.

----------------(1975). The Structure of Magic, Volume II. Palo Alto, California: Science and Behavior Books.----------------(1979). Frogs into Princes. Neuro-linguistic Programming. Moab, Utah: Real People Press.

----------------(1981). Trance-formations. Moab, Utah: Real People Press.

----------------(1982). Reframing – Neuro Linguistic Programming and the Transformation of Meaning. Moab, Utah: Real People Press.

Bandler, Richard & MacDonald, Will (1988). An Insider's Guide to Sub-Modalities. Cupertino, California: Meta Publications.

Bandler, Richard (1985). Using Your Brain for Change. Moab, Utah: Real People Press

Beck, Aaron; Rush, John; Shaw, Brian & Emory, Gary (1979). Cognitive Therapy of Depression. New York, N.Y.

Bentov, Itzhak (1977). Stalking the Wild Pendulum. On the Mechanics of Consciousness. Rochester, Vermont: Destiny Books

Bodenhamer, Bob & Hall, Michael L. (1998). Adventures with Time Lines. Capitola, California: Meta Publications.

----------------(1999). The User's Manual of the Brain, Volume One. Wales, UK: Crown House.

----------------(1999). The User's Manual of the Brain, Volume Two. Wales, UK: Crown House Publishing Limited.

Burns, David D., M.D. (1980). Feeling Good: The New Mood Therapy- Revised and Updated, Avon Books, Harper Collins Publishers. New York, N.Y.

Byron, T (1992). The Geo-cubic Matrix Flashing in the Universe and the Cosmos of Energy Matter Caught in its Time Flow Angels Camp, California: T.Bryon G Publishing

Capra, F. (1976) The Tao of Physics. New York, N.Y.: Bantam Books.

Damasio, A. (1994). Descarte's Error: Emotion, Reason and the Human Brain. New York, N.Y.: Grosset/Putnam.

----------------(2003). Looking for Spinoza, Joy, Sorrow and the Feeling Brain. New York, N.Y.: Harcourt Books.

Dolan, Yvonne M. (1991). Resolving Sexual Abuse, Solution Focused Therapy and Ericksonian Hypnosis for Adult Survivors. New York, N.Y.: W.W. Norton & Company.

----------------(1985). A Path with a Heart, Ericksonian Utilization with Resistant and Chronic Clients. New York, N.Y.: Brunner/Mazel.

Dunn, Jean (Editor) (1982). Seeds of Consciousness, The Wisdom of Sri Nisargadatta Maharaj. Durham, N.C.: Acorn Press.

----------------(1985). Prior to Consciousness, Talks With Sri Nisargadatta Maharaj. Durham, N.C.: Acorn Press.

----------------(1994). Consciousness & the Absolute, The Final Talks With Sri Nisargadatta Maharaj. Durham, N.C.: Acorn Press.

Erickson, Milton H. M.D. Edited by Ernest L Rossi & Margaret O. Ryan (1983). Healing in Hypnosis Volume I. New York, N.Y.: Irvington Publishers.

----------------(1985). Life Reframing in Hypnosis. New York, N.Y.: Irvington Publishers.

Erickson, Milton H., M.D. & Cooper, Lynn F (1959). Time Distortion in Hypnosis. New York, N.Y.: Irvington Publishers.

Erickson, M.H. and Rossi, E.L. (1989). The February Man, Evolving Consciousness and Facilitating New Identity in Hypnotherapy. New York, N.Y.: Brunner/Mazel.

Festinger, Leon (1957). A Theory of Cognitive Dissonance. Stanford CA: Stanford University Press.

Flint, Garry A Ph.D. (1999). Emotional Freedom. Vernon, B. C.: Neo Sol Terric Enterprises.

Foa, Edna B., Ph.D. &R. Reid Wilson, Ph.D. (1991). STOP Obsessing. New York, N.Y.: Bantam Books..

Fosha, Diana, Ph.D. (2000). The Transforming Power of Affect. New York, N. Y.: Basic Books.

Frankl, Viktor E. (1992). Search for Meaning: An Introduction to Logo Therapy. Boston, Massachusetts: Beacon Press.

French, Gerald D & Harris, Chrys J (1999). Traumatic Incident Reduction. Boca Ratan, Florida: CRC Press.

Gendlin, Eugene, Ph.D. (1978). Focusing. New York, N.Y.: Bantam Book.

Gibson, Eleanor, (1969). Principals of Perceptual Learning & Development. Englewood Cliffs, New Jersey: Prentice-Hall, Inc.

Gilligan, Stephen G. (1987). Therapeutic Trances. New York, N.Y.: Brunner/Mazel Publishers.

Glasser, William M.D. & Glasser, Carleen (1999). The Language of Choice Theory. New York, N. Y.: Harper Collins.

Gleick, James (1987). Chaos. New York, N. Y.: Penguin Books.

Golas, Thaddeus (1971). The Lazy Man's Guide to Enlightenment. New York. Bantam Books

Goleman, Daniel (1985). Vital Lives, Simple Truths. New York, N. Y.: Simon & Schuste.r

----------------(1995). Emotional Intelligence. New York, N. Y.: Bantam Books.

----------------(1988). The Meditative Mind: The Varieties of Meditative Experience, New York, N.Y.: Putnam Books.

Gordon, David C. (1978). Therapeutic Metaphors: Helping Others Through the Looking Glass. Capitola, California; Meta Publications.

Goulding, M.M. & Goulding, R.L. (1997). Changing Lives Through Redecision Therapy. (Revised Edition). New York, N.Y.: Grove.

Halevi, Z'ev Ben Shimon (1977). A Kabbalistic Universe. York Beach, Maine: Samuel Weiser, Inc.

Haley, Jay (1976). Problem Solving Therapy. San Francisco, California. Josey Bass Inc Publishers.

Hanh, Thich Nhat (1975). The Miracle of Mindfulness. Boston, Massachusetts: Beacon Press Books.

----------------(1988). The Heart of Understanding Commentaries on the Prajmaparamita Heart Sutra. Berkeley, California; Parallax Press.

----------------(1993). The Blooming of A Lotus. Boston, Massachusetts: Beacon Press

Havens, Ronald A., & Walters, Catherine, M.A. (1989). Hypnotherapy Scripts. New York, N.Y.: Brunner/Mazel Publishers.

Hellams, Wilton l., PhD. & Schreiber, Tobias S., M.A. (2006). "Mapping" Gifts from the Maps of Master Therapist. Moore, South Carolina. Eclectic Therapy Press.

Heller, Steven & Steele, Terry (1978). Monsters & Magical Sticks: There's No Such Thing As Hypnosis. Tempe, Arizona: New Falcon Publications.

Helmstetter, Shad (1987). The Self-Talk Solution. New York, N. Y.: William Morrow & Company, Inc.

Herbert, N. (1985). Quantum Reality. New York, N.Y.: Anchor Press.

Horner, Althea J. M.D. (1984). Object Relations and the Developing Ego in Therapy. North Vale, N. J.: Jason Aronson, Inc.

Hudson, Patricia O'Hanlon & O'Hanlon, William Hudson (1991). Rewriting Love Stories. New York: W. W. Norton & Co

Izard, C.E. (1977). Human Emotions. New York, N.Y.: Plenum.

James, T. & Woodsmall, W. (1988). Time Line Therapy and The Basis of Personality. Capitola, California: Meta Publications, Inc.

Johnson, Stephen M., (1994). Character Styles. New York, NY: W. W. Norton & Company.

Kaku, Michio (1994). Hyper-Space. New York: Double Day Anchor Book.

Kaplin, Aryeh (1990). Sefer Yetzirah. The Book of Creation. York Beach, Maine: Samuel Weiser, Inc.

Korzybski, A. (1993). Science and Sanity, An introduction to non-Aristotelian systems and general semantics (5th Edition). Brooklyn, N.Y.: Institute of General Semantics.

Krishnamurti, J (1996). Total Freedom. San Francisco, California: Harper Publishers.

Krishnamaruti, U.G. (1982. The Mystique of Enlightenment: The unrational Ideas of a man called U.G. India: Dinesh.

----------------(1988). The Mind is Myth. Disquieting Conversations with the Man called U.G.India: Dinesh Publications.

Kroeger, William S. (1977). Clinical and Experimental Hypnosis, Second Edition. Philadelphia, Pennsylvania: J. B. Lippincott Company.

Landis, Richard E (1991). Interactive Imageries For Habit, Feeling & Behavior Changes, Volume One, Self Re-parenting Guided Imageries. Laguna Niguel, California: Garrlitea Professional Publications.

Landis, Richard E (1991). Interactive Imageries for Habit, Feeling & Behavior changes, Volume Two: Parts-work. Santa Ana, California. Orange County Society of Ericksonian Professional Hypnosis Publications.

Lankton, Stephen R. & Lankton, Carol H. (1983). The Answer Within. New York, N. Y.: Brunner/Mazel, Inc.

Lankton, Stephen, ACSW (1980). Practical Magic. Cupertino, California: Meta Publications.

LeDoux, Joseph (1996). The Emotional Brain. New York, N. Y.: Simon & Schuster.

LeDoux, Joseph (2002). Synaptic Self. New York, N.Y.: Viking Penguin.

Levi, Eliphas (1984). The Book of Splendours. York Beach, Maine: Samuel Weiser, Inc.

Levine, Barbara H. (1991). Your Body Believes Every Word You Say. Boulder Creek, California: Asian Publishing Company.

Levine, Peter A., w/Anne Frederick (1997). Waking the Tiger, Healing Trauma. Berkeley, California: North Atlantic Books.

Maharaj, Nisargadatta, Sri (Translated by Maurice Frydeman) (1973). I Am That. Durham, N.C.: Acorn Press..

Maltz, Maxwell, M.D. (1973). Psycho-Cybernetics. North Hollywood, California: Wilshore Book Company.

Manfield, Phillip (Editor) (1998). Extending EMDR. New York, N.Y.: W. W. Norton & Company Inc.

Maultsby, Maxie C., Jr. (1990). Rational Behavior Therapy, Howard University-College of Medicine.

Mascaro', Juan (Translator) (1965). The Upanishads. New York, NY. Penguin Books.

McKay, Matthew, Fanning, Patrick (1991). Prisoners of Belief. Oakland, California: New Harbinger Publications Inc..

Napier, N. (1996). Recreating Yourself, Increasing Self Esteem through imaging, and Self Hypnosis. New York, N. Y.: Norton Publishers

O'Hanlon, William Hudson (1987). Tap Roots Underlying Principles of Milton Erickson's Therapy & Hypnosis. New York, N.Y.: W.W. Norton and Company.

O'Hanlon, William Hudson, Martin, Michael (1992) Solution Oriented Hypnosis. New York, N. Y.: W. W. Norton & Company.

Osborne, Arthur (Editor) (1972). The Collected Works of Ramana Maharshi. York Beach, Maine: Samuel Weiser, Inc.

Ouspensky, P. D. (1997). In Search of the Miraculous. Orlando, Florida: Harcourt Brace &Company.

Overdurf, John and Silverthorn, Julie (1994). Training Trances, Multi Level Communication In Therapy & Training. Portland, Oregon; Metamorphous Press.

Page, Michael, (1988). The Power of Chi. Thorsona, London: Aquarian Press

Parnell, Laurel, PhD. (2008). Tapping In. Boulder, CO. Sounds True, Inc.

Paulson, Genevieve Lewis (1993). Kundalini and the Chakras. St. Paul, Minnesota: Llewellyn Publications, Inc.

Pavlov, I.P. (1960). Conditioned Reflexes. New York, N.Y.: Dover (Original work published in 1927).

Pearson, Carol S. (1991). Awakening The Heroes Within. New York, NY: Harpers, Collins Publishers.

Perls, Fritz, M.D. (1992). Gestalt Therapy Verbatim.

Perls, Fritz (1942) Ego, Hunger and Aggression. Durban, South Africa.: Knox.

Perls, F. (1969) In and Out of the Garbage Pail. Moab, Utah: Real People Press.

Pert, Candace (1997) Molecules of Emotion. New York, NY: Scribner

Phillips, Maggie (2000). Finding the Energy to Heal. New York, N Y.: W. W. Norton & Company.

Piaget, Jean (2000). The Psychology of the Child. New York, N. Y.: Basic Books.

Powell, Robert (Editor) (1994). The Ultimate Medicine As Prescribed by Sri Nisargadatta Maharaj. San Diego, California: Blue Dove Press

----------------(1996. The Experience of Nothingness. San Diego, California: Blue Dove Press.

Prince, A. F. & Mou – Jay, Wong (1990). The Diamond Sutra, & The Sutra of Hui - Neng. Boston, Mass: Shambhala Press.

Putnam, F. W. (1989). Diagnoses and Treatment of Multiple Personality Disorder. New York, N.Y.: Guilford Press.

Raphael (1993). Pathway of Fire. York Beach, Maine: Samuel Weiser, Inc.

Resnikoff, Howard L. (1989). The Illusion of Reality. New York, N. Y.: Springer-Verlag.

Riso, Don Richard (1992). Discovering Your Personality Type. New York, N.Y.: Houghton Mifflin Company.

Rogers, Carl (1951). Client Centered Therapy. Boston, Massachusetts: Houghton Mifflin Company.

Rossi, E. L (1986) The Psychobiology of Mind Body Healing, New Concepts of Therapeutic Hypnosis. New York: N.Y.: W.W. Norton and Company.

Rothschild, Babette (2000). The Body Remembers: The Psychophysiology of Trauma and Treatment. New York, N.Y.: W.W. Norton and Company.

Schacter, D. (1996). Searching for Memory. New York, N.Y.: Basic Books.

Schore, Allan N (1994). Affect Regulation & the Origin of the Self – The Neurobiology of Emotional Development. Hillsdale, New Jersey; Lawrence Erlbaum Associates Publishers.

Schmidt, Shirley Jean (2002). Developmental Needs Meeting Strategy for EMDR Therapists. San Antonio, Texas.

Schultz, J. (1959). Autogenic Training. New York, N. Y.: Grune & Stratton Publishers.

Schwartz, Richard C. (1995). Internal Family Systems Therapy. New York, N. Y.: Guilford Press.

Selye, Hans (1984) The Stress of Life. New York, N.Y.: McGraw-Hill Publishers.

Shah, Idries (1964). The Sufis. New York, N. Y.: Double Day Publishers.

----------------(1978). Learning How to Learn: Psychology and Spirituality in the Sufis Way. San Francisco, California: Harper & Row.

----------------(1978). A Perfumed Scorpion: The Way to the Way. San Francisco, California: Harper & Row.

Shapiro, Francine, (2001). Eye Movement Desensitization and Reprocessing, Second Edition. New York, N.Y.: Guilford Press.

Shapiro, Francine (1995). Eye Movement Desensitization & Reprocessing. New York, NY: The Guilford Press.

Singh, Jaideva, (1980). The Divine Creative Pulsation. Delhi, India: Motilal Banarsidass Publishers.

----------------(1979). Siva Sutras. The Yoga of Supreme Identity. Delhi, Indiana: Motilal Banarsidass Publisher.

Speeth, Kathleen Riordan (1989). The Gurdjieff Work. New York, N. Y.: G. P. Putnam's Sons.

Spiegel, D. Editor (1993). Dissociative Disorders: A Clinical Review. Lutherville, Maryland: Sidran Press.

Spiegel, Herbert & Spiegel, David (1987). Trance and Treatment. New York, N.Y.: American Psychiatric Press Inc.

Starr, Kara (1989). Merlin's Journal of Time. Solana Beach, California: Raven Starr Publications

Stevens, John O. (1971). Awareness, Exploring Experimenting, Experiencing. New York: Bantam Books.

Stone, Hal & Sidra (1989). Embracing Ourselves. San Rafael, California: New World Library.

Stone, Hal & Sidra (1993). Embracing Your Inner Critic. New York, NY: Harper Collins Publishers.

Straus, Roger A., (1982). Strategic Self-Hypnosis. Englewood Cliffs, New Jersey: Prentice Hall, Inc.

Suares, Carlo (1992). The Cipher of Genesis. York Beach, Maine: Samuel Weiser, Inc.

Talbot, Michael (1988). Beyond the Quantum. New York, N. Y.: Bantam Books.----------------(1992). The Holographic Universe. New York, NY: Harper Perennial.

Tinker, R H. & Wilson, S. A. (1999). Through the Eyes of a Child: EMDR with Children. New York, N.Y.: Norton Publishers.

Tulka, Tarthang (1977). Time, Space and Knowledge. Berkeley, California: Dharma Publishing.

Tzu Lao translated by John Chu (1961). Tao Teh Ching. Boston, Massachusetts: Shambhala Publisher.

Van der Kolk, B. A., M.D. (1994). The Body Keeps the Score: Memory and the Evolving Psychobiology of Posttraumatic Stress. Harvard Review of Psychiatry.

Venkatesananda, Swami (Translator) (1976). The Supreme Yoga: A New Translation Volume 1, Himalayas, India, Tehri.

----------------(1976). The Supreme Yoga: A New Translation Volume 2. Himalayas, India, Tehri.

Watzlawick, Paul,; Weakland, John,ChE; and Fisch, Richard, M.D. (1974). Change Principles of Problem Formation and Problem Resolution. New York, N.Y...: W.W. Norton and Company.

W. Bill (2001). 4th Edition Big Book: World Services Inc.

Wilson, R. Reid (1986). Don't Panic: Taking Control of Anxiety Attacks. New York, NY: Harper & Row Publishers.

Wolf, Fred Allan (1988). Parallel Universes. New York, N. Y.: Simon & Schuster.

Wolinsky, Stephen (1996). Hearts on Fire, The Tao of Mediation. San Diego, California: Blue Dove Press.

----------------(1991. Trances Peoples Live. Las Vega, Nevada: Bramble Books.

----------------(1993). Quantum Consciousness. Las Vega, Nevada: Bramble Books.

----------------(1993). The Dark Side of the Inner Child. The Next Step. Norfolk, Connecticut: Bramble Books.

----------------(1994). The Tao of Chaos. BearsVille, New York: Bramble Books.

----------------(1999). The Way of the Human. Volume One. Capitola, California: Quantum Institute Press.

Wolinsky, Stephen (1999). The Way of the Human. Volume Three. Capitola, California. Quantum Institute Press.

----------------(1999). The Way of the Human. Volume Two. Capitola, California: Quantum Institute Press.

----------------(2000). Intimate Relationships. Capitola, California.

----------------(2000). I Am That I Am. Capitola, California: Quantum Institute Press.

----------------(2000). The Beginners Guide to Quantum Psychology. Capitola, California.

----------------(2002). You Are Not: Beyond the Three Veils of Consciousness. Capitola, California.

-----------------(2003). Walden III: In Search of A Utopian Nirvana. Capitola, California: Quantum Institute Press.
-----------------(2005). The Nirvana Sutras and Advaita-Vedanta. Capitola, California: Quantum Institute Press.

Video, DVD and Audio Material

Andreas, Steve & Connirae (1986). The Swish Pattern. DVD, Evergreen, Colorado: NLP Comprehensive.

Araoz, Daniel L. ED.D. (1984). Self-Transformation Through the New Hypnosis. Audio Cassette Series. New York, N.Y.: BMA Audio Cassette Publications.

Arntz, William (2004). What the Bleep Do We Know!? Twentieth Century Fox.

Cameron-Bandler, Leslie and Michael LeBeau (1984). NLP Video Tape, Home Study Program: Demonstrations of Patterns, 109 minute. Boulder, Colorado: Future Pace, Inc.

Klein, Ron (2000). Eye Movement Integration. Video Cassette: American Hypnosis Training Academy.

Levine, Peter A. (1999). Healing Trauma, Restoring the Wisdom of Your Body. 9 Hour Audio Cassette Series. Boulder, Colorado: Sounds True.

Orange County Society for Ericksonian Psychotherapy and Hypnosis (1978). Now You Wanted A Trance Demonstrated Today. Milton H. Erickson, M.D., Garden Grove, California: InfoMedix.

Wolinsky, Stephen (2004). I Am That I Am. DVD. www.netinetifilms.com

Wolinsky, Stephen (2006). Nirvana Means Extinction, I Am That I Am Part Two. DVD. www.netinetifilms.com

Wolinsky, Stephen (2007). I Am That I Am part III, Prior to Self Consciousness. DVD. www.netinetifilms.com

Wolinsky, Stephen (2002). Awakening From the Trance of Self, An Experiential Course on Developing Multidimensional Awareness. 9-hour audiocassette series. Boulder, Colorado: Sounds True. www.soundstrue.com

Wolinsky, Stephen (2008). Consciousness and Beyond. The Final Teachings of Sri Nisargadatta Maharaj. DVD. www.netinetifilms.com

Wolinsky, Stephen (2009).' The Inner Bhagavad-Gita "In the Light of Sri Nisargdatta Maharaj". www.netinetifilms.com

Yu, Ronny (2006). Fearless: Rogue Pictures.

Ayin/EnSof

It is Everything, It is Nothing

The silence is before, after, and behind the words